Roger Zelazny: A Primary and Secondary Bibliography

Masters of
Science Fiction and Fantasy

Editor
L. W. Currey

Advisory Aquisitions Editor
Marshall B. Tymn

Roger Zelazny: A Primary and Secondary Bibliography

Joseph L. Sanders

G.K.HALL&CO.

70 LINCOLN STREET, BOSTON, MASS.

Library of Congress Cataloging in Publication Data

Sanders, Joseph L
  Roger Zelazny, a primary and secondary bibliography.

  Includes indexes.
  1. Zelazny, Roger, 1937-   --Bibliography.
I. Title.
Z8997.829.S26 [PS3576.E43] 016.813'54   80-20253
ISBN 0-8161-8081-4

This publication is printed on permanent/durable acid-free paper
MANUFACTURED IN THE UNITED STATES OF AMERICA

To My Mother Mary Frances Sanders

And My Wife Mary Elizabeth Sanders

Contents

Introduction

Roger Joseph Zelazny was born in Cleveland, Ohio, on May 13, 1937, the only child of Joseph Frank Zelazny and Josephine (Sweet) Zelazny. Roger attended Noble School (1943-1949) in Euclid, a Cleveland suburb. He began reading science fiction when he was 10 or 11, and he also began writing at an early age--partly for his private satisfaction, partly in competition with others. During his years at Shore Junior High School (1949-1952) in Euclid, Zelazny engaged in a protracted writing contest with his classmate Carl Yoke.[1] This exchange of boasts and insults included a series of stories about two sloppy but crafty monsters, Zlaz and Yok, who amble in and out of outrageous situations--the closest descendent of these stories in Zelazny's published fiction is probably "The Great Slow Kings." A surviving sample in Yoke's possession indicates that writing the series aided the development of Zelazny's skills, for it is a well constructed and cleverly written effort for a young writer.

In Euclid Senior High School (1952-1955), Zelazny continued his writing. After taking a journalism class during his junior year under Myron Gordon, he became news editor for the school newspaper in his senior year. During his junior year he had also joined the Creative Writing Club under the direction of Ruby Olson. Both teachers encouraged Zelazny in his writing. Mrs. Olson especially praised his poetry. His stories and poems

appeared in the high school literary magazine, and he
sold one of the stories to Literary Cavalcade. The bulk
of this early fiction was science fiction or fantasy.
Beginning in 1955, some of Zelazny's stories were published in fanzines, the small-edition amateur magazines
put out by science fiction fans, but the stories he submitted to professional science fiction magazines at that
time were rejected. Zelazny was writing mainly poetry
by the time he was 18.

After beginning his studies at Western Reserve University, Cleveland, as a psychology major, Zelazny
switched to English in his senior year. Several poems
and a short parable were published in the college literary magazine. He won the Finley Foster Poetry Award
twice (1957 and 1959) for groups of poems, and the
Holden Essay Award once (1959) for a rewritten term
paper on Chaucer.

During 1959-1960, Zelazny attended Columbia University as a master's candidate in English and Comparative
Literature. He left New York in 1960 and joined the
Ohio National Guard, serving his six-month tour of ac-
tive duty primarily in Texas and at the same time pre-
paring his Master's thesis, an examination of morality
and humor comedy conventions in The Revenger's Tragedy. He received his degree from Columbia in 1962.
Sometime early in his graduate school years, Zelazny
submitted a collection of poems, "Chisel in the Sky," to
the Yales Series of Younger Poets contest. The manuscript's failure to win convinced him to try prose writing again.

In the early 1960s Zelazny returned to science
fiction. In addition to his greater maturity, he had
gained some specific assets over the years: a literary
education built on much personal reading and increased
to the point of saturation, especially in Elizabethan or
Jacobean drama, at graduate school: and an athletic pro-
ficiency in certain physical sports that gave his action

scenes special solidness and believability. Also, his skills of observation were being sharpened by his new job as a Social Security interviewer:

> I looked at people's hands and the gestures they made with them. I studied their faces, wondered about their clothing, their jewelry, their scars. I listened to them lie and tell what they thought was the truth.[2]

Finally, a not inconsiderable advantage, Zelazny came to science fiction without the overwhelming familiarity that sometimes binds new efforts to the shape of known works. He had read little science fiction of recent years, and he approached the field with an outsider's freshness, as well as with affection.

Zelazny's procedure in seeing whether he could write science fiction professionally was to write one story an evening and to polish it the following night. He drew up a list of suitable magazines with the exception of Analog (since he was sure that John W. Campbell would not care for the kind of story he intended to write) and sent batches of completed stories to the first magazine on the list. When the stories came back, he sent them to the next magazine, and so on down the list. Since the list was arranged alphabetically, Amazing happened to be first. After a short time, Cele Goldsmith, editor of Amazing and Fantastic, added encouraging notes to the rejection slips. Slightly more than a month after Zelazny began sending stories around, Goldsmith bought "Passion Play," and a week and a half later she bought another story. Of the seventeen stories Zelazny sold in his first year of writing, Goldsmith bought fourteen. Remembering her encouragement, Zelazny says that "It wasn't anything in particular that Cele said, so much as the fact that she treated me like a professional from the very beginning."[3]

Zelazny's ultimate goal, of course, was to become a full-time professional writer. He was delayed by several factors. On one hand, his government job was time-consuming; on the other it provided a steady, dependable income whereas the prospects of free-lance writing were uncertain. At the same time, some disturbing events shook Zelazny's personal life. His father died on November 25, 1964, and not long before, Zelazny had been injured in an automobile accident in which his fiancée Sharon Steberl was so seriously injured that their wedding had to be postponed until late 1964.[4] The marriage proved to be an unfortunate one; they separated late in the summer of 1965 and were divorced June 27, 1966. About the same time, Zelazny moved to Baltimore, Maryland. His output at this time--"He Who Shapes," "The Doors of His Face, The Lamps of His Mouth," and other fine stories--was astonishing under the circumstances.

His first two novels, This Immortal and The Dream Master, were published in 1966. On August 20 of that year he married Judith Alene Callahan. For the next several years he continued to publish short fiction and some novels of high quality, culminating in Lord of Light in 1967. By this time Zelazny had acquired a considerable reputation as a writer and had developed his marketing skills. He resigned from the Social Security Administration in 1969 and began writing full time. He now switched from shorter to longer pieces of fiction. At the beginning of his career, Zelazny had focused on short stories because they fitted into the slack periods of his working schedule and he could afford to keep numerous stories circulating until they sold. Later, with a mastery of fiction and a marketable reputation, he was able to obtain advance contracts for novels and thus could provide a more predictable income for his family.

Zelazny has settled comfortably into the life of a full-time author. The birth of his two sons, Devin Joseph in 1971 and Jonathan Trent in 1976, has nudged a long-standing desire to write books for children. In

1975 he and his family moved from Baltimore to Santa Fe,
New Mexico, where he has explored new background and
local history that already have shown up in such works
as Bridge of Ashes.

He continues to read widely in the sciences and to
travel to interesting conventions. And to write.

Zelazny's work has received numerous awards and nominations (see Appendix A). In addition, to quote his
own 1977 vita,

> His speaking engagements have included
> the Maryland Institute, the Smithsonian
> Associates, the University of Maryland,
> the Indiana University Writers' Confer-
> ence, the Science Fiction Research Asso-
> ciation Conference at Penn State, the
> Maryland Council for the Social Sciences
> Spring Conference, "From Global Through
> Personal Future Alternatives to 2000 and
> Beyond," the Science Fiction Fantasy &
> Fact Conference at Kean College, New
> Jersey; UCLA's "Ten Tuesdays Down a Rab-
> bit Hole: The World of Science Fiction,"
> visiting lecturer and writer-in-residence
> at Justin Morrill College, Michigan State
> University, Clarion Science Fiction Writ-
> ers Workshop, the Kent State University
> Author-Lecture Series, the University of
> California at Irvine, Oklahoma University
> and Midwestern State University.

His taped readings of his own works, "The Doors of His
Face, the Lamps of His Mouth" and "Love is an Imaginary
Number," were broadcast over Pacifica radio stations in
1967 and 1968, as was his reading of a selection of contemporary poetry. He served as secretary-treasurer of
the Science Fiction Writers of America from 1967 to
1968. He has been guest of honor at several conventions,

including the 1975 World Science Fiction Convention in Washington, D.C., Ozarkcon 4, and the MileHiCon in Denver in 1977.

And this is probably as deep as a biographical sketch should go into Zelazny's background. Zelazny is, despite his immense considerateness of others, a very private person. As he says in the "interview" he conducted with himself for Paul Walker,

> I like to keep my writing apart from the rest of my life. I make my living displaying pieces of my soul in some distorted form or other. The rest of it is my own. . . . Communication is generally a form of self-expression, but the opposite does not necessarily apply. I consider myself in the communication business, not the self-expression business. They are necessarily bound up together in any piece of fiction, but I put in only as much of myself as I deem appropriate, no more, no less. If the story is a failure, it is not worth much consideration; if it is successful, then everything is in place, and it should not be necessary to ask for more.[5]

Rationalization though this may be in part, it is a reasonable position. Let us, therefore, turn to a consideration of Zelazny's fiction and the critical response it has received.

THEMES AND CRITICISM

As the lengthy bibliography of criticism in Part D, Critical Studies, shows, Zelazny has received considerable attention from readers ranging from letters to the editor early in his career (summarized in D1) to several dissertations, and now to a book-length critical study

and a full-scale bibliography. Much of this attention
has been favorable, and even the negative criticism has
expressed a high regard for Zelazny's ability. Some
critics, however, have voiced irritation when Zelazny
has not done exactly what they expected, even though
they may have misinterpreted his work. The two most
serious misinterpretations, which show up repeatedly
in the critical studies surveyed in Part D, concern
Zelazny's use of myth and his prose style.

Many critics who have identified mythical allusions
and echoes in Zelazny's work have wondered whether each
reference masks a hidden message, or whether the allusions are merely a playful literary decoration. As a
result, Zelazny has at different times been both hailed
as a creator of new myths for our time and dismissed for
his outgrown, unworkable clichés. Such critics fail to
understand the nature of myth or how Zelazny uses myth.

On the surface, Zelazny uses mythic references to
create what he calls "a resonance-effect" in the reader,
as he explains in comments on his adventure novel
Damnation Alley:

> I think that if someone has had even a
> brief exposure to a particular medium,
> something that later mimes it will strike
> a chord of familiarity, even if he does
> not know why, even if, say, his only ex-
> posure to Noh was forgotten background
> sequences in Sayonara. A sense of famil-
> iarity is always a good thing to stir in
> a reader, as I see it, perhaps especially
> when he doesn't know why. It makes a
> thing seem somehow more important if it
> nags him a bit.[6]

In the same way, mythic allusion presumably can reach
even the reader whose knowledge of myth stems from reading a kindergarten story book or from glancing at tele-
vision's Shazam on Saturday mornings, and such allusions

will give the story extra resonance, a nagging sense of "importance."

Zelazny makes the large assumption that any contact with myth will lead us to recognize at least this sense of importance when references to myths appear in other contexts. He does so, I believe, with the confidence that classic literature survives because it still speaks to the human predicament, that human yearnings are similar enough to reach across the boundaries of culture and of time--and that, by extension, ancient myths still have power to hold the reader's attention and involve him in a sense of "important" action.

What is a myth? Why, bereft of factual import, does it survive? Because myth represents a recurring pattern of human experience, summed up in a particular set of circumstances and names; its appeal and its power lie in the fact that mythic forms suddenly leap out at us from the flow of events in our lives. Recognizing myth's similarity to our own experience clarifies and deepens our understanding of what is happening to us. Myth comforts us by suggesting that what we are experiencing is not absolutely unique, and it gives us a sense of control over the pattern we now see distinctly.

This view of myth suggests that the patterns therein are rigid and unchangeable. Mythical characters are therefore constant, now and forever. Consider how John Henry, for example, predicts his fate while sitting on his daddy's knee. Consider how, in the mythical aspect of Christianity, the infant Christ stares at the beholder from his mother's arms in pre-Renaissance paintings as a stern little Lord of the Universe. Just as myths express timeless truth in the patterns of perception and behavior they depict, so do the characters of myth partake of and represent the changeless nature of those truths. James Blish refers to this aspect of myth when he attacks Zelazny for using the names of the Egyptian gods in <u>Creatures of Light and Darkness</u> and for

Introduction

thus invoking "the whole complex of associations which
goes with them, the static assumptions of a fixed cosmos
about which everything important is already known."[7]

The other implication of this view of myth is that
right and wrong are fixed moral standards, and that
characters and actions can be easily labeled good or
evil. To be sure, characters like Loki or Judas may de-
ceive others for a time, but ultimately they will be
judged by the wise, self-knowing characters around them.

With these points in mind, we can examine how
Zelazny uses myth, which is _not_ in accordance with the
limitations noted above. Zelazny's myths certainly do
not fit Franz Rottensteiner's description: "crutches
for an unoriginal mind turning to the past because it is
either unwilling or unable to come to grips with the
realities of the present or a probable future."[8] Rather
than clinging to a myth for security, Zelazny boldly
shatters myth and throws away many vital parts; rather
than holding to a fixed sense of character and morality,
his stories rejoice in the invigorating, mind-straining
process of self-discovery and moral growth that myth can
stimulate.

A number of critics have missed the point of
Zelazny's references to mythical gods. The characters
who proclaim their divine identities in works such as
Creatures of Light and Darkness and Lord of Light, for
example, are not meant to be taken for gods themselves.
They are human beings trying to play the roles of gods.
The stories hint at a technological basis for the
"gods'" vast powers, but it also becomes clear that
those beings are not quite omnipotent and they certainly
are not omniscient. Zelazny's point, surely, is that
the role differs from the person trying to fill it.
Zelazny lets the reader make that deduction by letting
him see characters with the names of gods behave and
speak in mundane ways. He sees them try to fill the
role, and he sees them fail. Characters who believe they

deserve to fill the role of gods, like the deicrats in
Lord of Light, are at best foolish, at worst foolishly
self-destructive.

Whether or not Zelazny's characters go so far as to
assume they actually are gods, if they cling to myth
they always destroy themselves. The Martians in "A Rose
for Ecclesiastes" are set on the path of self-destructive
adherence to a set, mythic role by an historical disas-
ter; Render and Elaine Shallot in The Dream Master are
destroyed by their personal inadequacies. However, the
flight from personal responsibility that leads an individual to sieze a set role because it may resemble
his desired state of mind means that any characteristics
unimportant to the role must be suppressed. As situa-
tions in life change along with the circumstances that
made the individual think he could play a mythic role,
he finds that in order to keep up the role he must deny
reality and his genuine self. That way leads only to
madness, sterility, and death.

On the other hand, many of Zelazny's main characters
are role players in a different sense, in that they con-
sciously decide to play a part for a limited time in
order to achieve a particular goal. They may let other
people believe they are gods, but they themselves know
better. Even when they discover satisfying--or gen-
uinely revealing--aspects of their role, they are not
sucked into it permanently because they recognize the
fragility of the power that a myth gives its servant.
Thus, as it usually happens, when they discover that
their supposed real identity is itself only transitory,
they are free to grow beyond it and not doomed to shrink
into mythic patterns. Carl Yoke has suggested that
Zelazny's work adapts literary conventions[9] by redirect-
ing them from the inside until they prove to be utterly
different from the original. In the same way, Zelazny's
"myths" are broken to the extent that Zelazny's characters are sane and strong enough to escape from the
static aspects of myth.

The impermanence of character in Zelazny's fiction is accompanied by an impermanence of value. Certainly there are no gods to give man a set of rules by which to live. The only gods who actually appear on stage, at the conclusion of Isle of The Dead, have a sense of morality so unlike that of human beings that we can learn nothing of moral value from them. In general, Zelazny writes about characters who have to get along without gods. As Zelazny tactfully explained to a Catholic priest who had sent him a student's paper on his fiction, his books

> were written with the notion of a vision of Deity as basically unknowable by man, save for possible instances of personal revelation, mystical experience, private Epiphany, which in themselves would serve to enlighten only the recipients, remaining essentially incommunicable by them to other men. In the absence of such a situation the individual who conceives of Deity at all must necessarily achieve his faith or ideas on the basis of hearsay, guesswork or lines of reasoning which derive from assailable premises. In this case, a lack of proper knowledge is necessarily companion to a lack of knowledge as to what is truly proper. Seen in this light, the act of praising God then comes to involve such presumption on the part of the praiser that it might well in itself be a form of blasphemy.[10]

Indeed, the "good guys" in Zelazny's work often engage in downright despicable behavior. Zelazny's heroes usually are depicted with words that traditionally denote evil. In Lord of Light, for example, Sam speaks of planning "sins," and of "attacking Heaven," but this association with evil is primarily a verbal one, since the "gods," as noted above, are fallible human beings who

play at being gods and who must be stopped before they
do great damage. Although other characters are more
difficult to sympathize with, their behavior seems to
fit the moment. Jack of Shadows, who deserves his nick-
name Jack of Evil, seems to act correctly in destroying
the static system of his world and in restoring it to
motion. And at the conclusion of the Amber series,
Corwin avoids single combat with Borel and kills him
treacherously not so much because he is afraid of Borel
but because he has too much else of importance to do;
as he says, "This isn't exactly the Olympic Games."[11]

An end may justify the means--if it is important
enough. Sometimes the means are far more important than
any end; sometimes only particular means can lead to a
discovery of the end's true value. In Zelazny's stories,
right and wrong form a confusing tangle, altering as
circumstances alter. Myth does not really help to re-
solve the confusion.

If Zelazny's purpose is not to refurbish myth, what
is it? As the above discussion suggests, Zelazny is.
deeply concerned with character and morality. His basic
subject is the growth of character, through role playing, philosophical dialogue, bloody action, and other
forms of behavior, from a particular personality at the
beginning of a story into a fuller one at the end, and a
recognition that it, too, will evolve into another personality, for it is simply one state in an unending
process of growth. (If, like many of Zelazny's heroes,
the hero is immortal, the process of creative change may
literally be unending.) Some critics have objected to
the apparent confusion of Zelazny's plots, particularly
in the Amber books. But surely this is a deliberate
mechanism on Zelazny's part to show that the characters
feel much the same way. The action is confusing for
even the schemers like Corwin, whose plans are countered
by unexpected events, and Oberon, master plotter, whose
hopes for the throne's succession are thwarted. In the

end, Corwin settles for less than perfect knowledge and
control as he evaluates himself, speaking in the third
person:

> He would like to think that he has learned
> something of trust, that he has washed his
> eyes in some clear spring, that he has
> polished an ideal or two. Never mind. He
> may still be only a smart-mouthed meddler,
> skilled mainly in the minor art of survival,
> blind as ever the dungeons knew him to the
> finer shades of irony. Never mind, let it
> to, let it be. I may never be pleased with
> him.[12]

We do not, Zelazny suggests, need a happy ending. We
may not need anything as conclusive as an "ending" at
all. Instead, perhaps we can learn to rejoice in what
Sam preaches to the monks in the first chapter of Lord
of Light: a struggle to create beauty and order out of
the ugly purposelessness of life. Zelazny's heroes
fight to make the world safe for uncertainty.

This struggle, suggests Zelazny's major theme. It
is possible, as I have done elsewhere, to trace this
idea throughout the basic plot structure that recurs in
his fiction.[14] But Zelazny also has shown great willingness to vary that structure in order to ensure his
artistic growth. As he explains,

> In every book that I have written to date,
> I have attempted something different--a
> structural effect, a particular character-
> ization, a narrative or stylistic method--
> which I have not used previously. It
> always involves what I consider my weak
> points as a writer, rather than my strong
> points. These efforts are for the pur-
> poses of improving my skills and abilities.[14]

Zelazny's theme closely resembles his own efforts as a writer. It cannot be coincidental that "shadows," the source of Jack's power and the material out of which the royal family of Amber creates its wonderful worlds, is the same word that Zelazny himself uses to describe "what lies between the pictures"--the undescribed areas in a work of literature that permit the audience to use its imagination to embellish, enrich, and fall deeper and deeper into rapport with the work. As he presses himself to extend his range as an imaginer, he shows characters whose comprehension is being strained beyond comfortable limits--but not, amazingly, beyond their true range. Like Browning, Zelazny believes that one should reach for more than he can grasp. Zelazny preaches that philosophy and practices it. Thus, Zelazny's beliefs can be seen in his creations more effectively than biography can explain.

With Zelazny's themes in mind let us consider his style, the second most misunderstood element of his work. We should not be surprised to find Zelazny's purpose reflected in his prose style. A number of reviewers and critics have singled it out as especially offensive or delightful. Those who dislike it are distressed to hear current slang from the mouths of gods or to hear high, formal diction in one sentence and breezy street talk in the next. Those who like Zelazny's style find it a joy in itself (even if they delight in the intellectual emptiness of science fiction)[15] or justify it as a suitable method of showing the varied experiences and interests of Zelazny's characters.[16]

This last observation has merit. Just as Zelazny's characters represent change and defy neat (mythic) labeling, so his style expresses disorder and defies simple analysis. In the Amber series, for example, Corwin's mixture of colloquial and poetic diction serves to elevate, then lower both Corwin's subject and the character himself. He is a sage immortal; he is an immature smartass; he is both; he is neither; he is himself.

Introduction

What Zelazny attempts to do is break readers out of
their preconceptions so they can respond to what is
truly important in experience, including language, and
not settle comfortably into one mode of reading.

Zelazny's vivid descriptions can even create be-
lievable impossibilities. For example, "A Rose for
Ecclesiastes," which was written after science had es-
tablished that the Mars depicted in this story was sci-
entifically impossible, was a deliberate homage to the
tradition of stories set on an inhabitable Mars. Yet,
the story is convincing. This regard for science fiction's past suggests that Zelazny's fiction does not
entirely tear myth to shreds and throw the pieces away,
but that he can put new life into literary and mythical
allusions and that out of the past he can take a cliché
like "the peace that passeth understanding"[17] and can
make it fresh and true.

Consider how the images that Banks Mebane labels
Zelazny's metaphysical images make us aware of connections between the familiar and the new, giving us a
richer sense of reality. This interpretation fits
Samuel Delaney's comment about the outlook of immortal
characters in Zelazny's work:

> Given all eternity to live, each experience
> becomes a jewel in the jewel-clutter of
> life; each moment becomes infinitely fasci-
> nating because there is so much more to
> relate to it; each event will take on new
> harmonies as it is struck by the overtones
> of history and lives experienced before.
> The most dour and colorless happening will
> be illuminated by the light of the ages.
> This is the raison behind the hallucinated,
> intensely symbolic language.[18]

So Zelazny is not simply discarding the past. The
past--literary allusions, large or small chunks of myth,

vividly revitalized verbal formulas--mixes with the ornate word play and straightforward, clipped declarative sentences characteristic of his work to create a new, vital entity. Zelazny's style is another manifestation of his major theme, that all life is a process of making and dissolving. In the Amber series, as Corwin finally comes to understand, life exists between two poles, Pattern and Chaos. Neither "wins." The difficult, creative tension between them continues, just as life continues. And Zelazny's style reflects that idea.

A number of the reviewers and/or critics listed here have seen this tension or part of it. Some also have touched on what seems to me the strongest criticism of Zelazny's fiction: for all the verbal invocations of love and the sensitive but indirect way love is treated in Lord of Light, it seldom is presented convincingly there. Zelazny's women tend to be ideals--or one particular ideal--rather than persons. The growing, maturing individual does not find a growing maturing relationship with anyone else. It may be, as Zelazny's long-time friend and reader Carl Yoke suggests, that before a man can love anyone else he must fully accept himself and his past, without being trapped by these boundaries. So perhaps what we see in Zelazny's work is a character becoming capable of a relationship that is not yet seen.[19]

Working within definite boundaries himself, Zelazny has shown a willingness to forego the safe and predictable effects that would have kept readers comfortable. The criticism in Part D shows the irritation and bafflement that his work has caused. It also shows the appreciation that he has received. Doubtless he has earned both. Better understanding of Zelazny's efforts should lead to greater appreciation of what he is trying to accomplish, as well as increased admiration for what he already has done so spendidly.

Introduction

TEXTUAL MATTERS

I have used relatively few abbreviations in the following pages, most of which should be self-evident, for example, F&SF for The Magazine of Fantasy and Science Fiction, If for Worlds of If, DAI for Dissertation Abstracts International, and so on. Periodicals with acronyms in the title include WSFA Journal (Washington Science Fiction Association) and SFWA Forum (Science Fiction Writers of America).

Items marked with an asterisk have not been examined by me. The introductory note for each part indicates primary sources of information used in constructing such entries; other sources of information appear with the particular entry.

In the case of fanzines, I generally have given issue numbers rather than volume numbers, since most fanzines actually are published by single issue, whatever the editor's pretentions. I have used volume numbers only if the fanzine insists. Most inconsistencies in the handling of number, dating, title, and other details of the fanzines I have seen are present in the original issues.

NOTES

1. This section is based on information directly from Yoke and Zelazny himself, or from correspondence files. The information is so thoroughly mingled here that I give sources only for direct quotes.

2. Statement written for Galaxy Publishing Corporation, in the Roger Zelazny Collection, George Arents Research Library at Syracuse University, no date.

3. Letter to Joe Sanders, 4 October 1974. Also letter to Ralph Anderson, 19 September 1971 (University of Maryland, Baltimore County Collection).

4. Discussed by Thomas F. Monteleone, "Science Fiction as Literature: Selected Stories and Novels of Roger Zelazny" (Master's thesis, University of Baltimore, 1973), p. 66. Monteleone identifies this as the source of the accident that forms part of The Dream Master's conclusion, as well as the distrust of cars that shows up in Zelazny's other fiction.

5. Published as "an Interview With Roger Zelazny," Luna Monthly [fanzine], No. 43 (December 1973), pp. 1-2.

6. Letter to Carl B. Yoke, quoted in Yoke's "Zelazny's Damnation Alley: Hell Noh," Extrapolation, 15 (December 1973), 6.

7. Review of Creatures of Light and Darkness, F & SF, 38 (April 1970), 51.

8. Review of A Rose for Ecclesiastes and Isle of the Dead, Speculation [fanzine], No. 26 (May 1970), p. 29.

9. Yoke, "Zelazny's Damnation Alley."

10. Letter to Reverend Flynn, 4 May 1973. In the collection of Zelazny's papers at the University of Maryland, Baltimore County Collection.

11. The Courts of Chaos (Garden City, New York: Doubleday, 1978), p. 132.

12. Ibid., pp. 131-132.

13. "Zelazny: Unfinished Business," in Voices for the Future, II, ed. Thomas D. Clareson (Bowling Green, Ohio: Bowling Green University Press, 1979), pp. 183-184.

14. In "Up Against the Wall, Roger Zelazny," an interview by Jeffrey D. Smith, additional questions by Richard E. Geis, The Alien Critic [fanzine], No. 7 (November 1973), p. 35.

15. Michael Wood, "Coffee Break for Sisyphus," Review of <u>Sign of the Unicorn</u>, <u>The New York Review of Books</u>, 22 (2 October 1975), 7.

16. James Blish, Review of <u>Nine Princes in Amber</u>, <u>F & SF</u>, 40 (May 1971), 39.

17. <u>Lord of Light</u> (Garden City, N.Y.: Doubleday, 1967), p. 9.

18. "Faust and Archimedes," <u>SFWA Forum</u> (August 1969), p. 21.

19. Conversation with Carl Yoke, 3 January 1978.

Acknowledgments

This bibliography attempts to list the available writings by and about Roger Zelazny. Obviously it draws on the work of other researchers, chiefly the indexes to science fiction magazines published by the New England Science Fiction Association. An inspection of the manuscript of William Contento's Index to Science Fiction Anthologies and Collections (Boston: G. K. Hall, 1978), in the possession of Lloyd W. Currey, also supplied much vital information for Part A. Hal Hall's Science Fiction Book Review Index proved essential in compiling the critical studies of Zelazny's work. I have verified all information by personal inspection whenever possible, and I have added information from my own research.

Beyond checking obvious sources, I have attempted to find solid information on the material Zelazny generously donated to fanzines--some of which has been reprinted several times in other fanzines but some of which even Zelazny has forgotten. Lacking any central index--or repository--of fanzines, I have found this a very frustrating task. I am resigned to the fact that somewhere, in a hectographed Bulgarian apazine, may be found the definitive analysis of Lord of Light.

A number of people have helped make this work as thorough and reliable as it is. First of all, I must thank several science fiction fans: Buck and Juanita Coulson, and Don and Maggie Thompson for advice and some well-aimed introductions; Mark Owings, Dennis Lien, Douglas Barbour, and Mike Glyer for answering my letters of inquiry with

valuable clues; Sandra Miesel, Bruce Pelz, Alex Eisen-
stein, Jeff Smith, and Hank and Lesleigh Luttrell for
searching through their fanzine collections; and Howard
DeVore and Ben Jason for helping me locate magazine references in their science fiction collections. I must
also thank Hal Hall for valuable information; Thomas F.
Monteleone for help with an earlier project that I was
able to incorporate; Carl Yoke for much information,
especially about Zelazny's early life and writing; the
archivists at Case Western Reserve University for checking the work Zelazny published while he was a student at
Case; the library staff of the George Arents Research
Library at Syracuse University for helping me to accomplish a great deal in my short visit before the 1978
blizzard; Binnie S. Brunstein of the University of
Maryland Baltimore County Library, a Zelazny fan and a
prompt supplier of information; and Lloyd and Alida
Currey for their hospitality and their aid in using the
remarkable research facilities at L. W. Currey Rare
Books. Very special thanks go to Roger Zelazny, whose
courtesy and good humor never failed throughout the many
queries and manuscript material I sent to him.

                                        Mentor, Ohio
                                        Spring 1979

Bibliography

Part A: Fiction

Part A lists Zelazny's fiction printed in English, in both professional and amateur publications. For items I have examined, page numbers indicate actual beginning and concluding pages of text—i.e., a full page illustration facing the opening page of text is not included in these page numbers, even though the magazine's table of contents may indicate that the story begins with the page of illustration. Items are arranged chronologically by date of publication, alphabetically if published simultaneously. Brief comments, along with items such as conjectural dates and page numbers, are enclosed in brackets.

1953

A1   "Conditional Benefits," Thurban I [fanzine], no. 3 (August-September), pp. 6-8. ["1st part of two-part serial--short story--of which 2nd part never appeared because the editor was drafted and the (fan)zine folded; I was assistant editor (of this issue)"--Zelazny.]

1954

A2   "And the Darkness is Harsh," Eucuyo [Euclid High School literary magazine], p. 33.

A3   "Mr. Fuller's Revolt," <u>Eucuyo</u> [Euclid High School
     literary magazine], pp. 7-8. [Zelazny also sold
     this story to <u>Literary Cavalcade</u> (the <u>National
     Scholastic</u> high school magazine), 7 (October
     1954), 29-30; the $25 he received was his first
     payment for writing--Zelazny.]

                          1955

A4   "Youth Eternal," <u>Eucuyo</u> [Euclid High School lit-
     erary magazine], pp. 20-21.

                          1958

A5   "The Outward Sign," <u>Skyline</u> [Western Reserve Uni-
     versity literary magazine], 31 (April), pp. 6-7.

                          1962

A6   "Horseman!" <u>Fantastic</u>, 11 (August), 109-111.

     *J. C. Reid, ed. <u>40 Short Short Stories</u>. London:
      Edward Arnold, 1965. [British school text--
      Zelazny.]

A7   "Passion Play," <u>Amazing</u>, 36 (August), 31-33.

     <u>Great Science Fiction</u>, no. 8 (1967). [Like most
        of the curiously titled periodicals reprinting
        Zelazny's early work, this was an elusive and
        irregular digest-sized magazine reprinted di-
        rectly from the pages of the Ziff-Davis publi-
        cations, <u>Amazing</u> and <u>Fantastic</u>, resulting from
        the acquisition of reprint rights by the new
        publisher. They are identical to the originals
        in text.]

                           4

A8   "The Teachers Rode a Wheel of Fire," Fantastic,
     11 (October), 108-112.

A9   "Moonless in Byzantium," Amazing, 36 (December),
     35-39.

     The Most Thrilling Science Fiction Ever Told,
        no. 7 (Winter 1967).

                        1963

A10 "On the Road to Splenoba," Fantastic, 12
     (January), 115-122.

A11 "Final Dining," Fantastic, 12 (February), 77-84.

A12 "The Borgia Hand," Amazing, 37 (March), 73-76.

     SF Greats, no. 21 (Spring 1971).

A13 "Nine Starships Waiting," Fantastic, 12 (March),
     98-125.

     Strange Fantasy, no. 8 (Spring 1969).

A14 "Circe Has Her Problems," Amazing, 37 (April),
     70-75.

     *Great Science Fiction from Amazing, no. 3 (n.d.).

A15 "The Malatesta Collection," Fantastic, 12 (April),
     47-52.

     Ted White, ed. The Best from Fantastic. New
        York: Manor, 1973 [paper].

A16 "The Stainless Steel Leech" [Harrison Denmark,
     pseud], Amazing, 37 (April), 115-118.

A17   "A Thing of Terrible Beauty" [Harrison Denmark, pseud], Fantastic, 12 (April), 75-80.

A18   "Monologue for Two" [Harrison Denmark, pseud], Fantastic, 12 (May), 110-111.

A19   "Threshold of the Prophet," Fantastic, 12 (May), 67-71.

A20   "A Museum Piece," Fantastic, 12 (June), 119-127.

       Strange Fantasy, no. 9 (Summer 1969).
       Terry Carr, ed. New Worlds of Fantasy #2. New York: Ace, 1970 [paper].
       In The Doors of His Face, The Lamps of His Mouth, and Other Stories, 1971.
       Thomas F. Monteleone, ed. The Arts and Beyond. Garden City, N.Y.: Doubleday, 1977.
       Fantastic Science Fiction, 27 (July 1979). [Another unauthorized reprint, this one reset. See A7.]

A21   "Mine is the Kingdom" [Harrison Denmark, pseud.], Amazing, 37 (August), 108-120.

A22   "King Solomon's Ring," Fantastic, 12 (October), 49-67, 98.

       Great Science Fiction, no. 11 (Summer 1968).
       Terry Carr, ed. On Our Way to the Future. New York: Ace, 1970 [paper].

A23   "The Misfit," Amazing, 37 (October), 116-119.

       Most Thrilling Science Fiction Ever Told, no. 8 (Spring 1968).
       Ted White, ed. The Best from Amazing. New York: Manor, 1973 [paper].

A24   "A Rose for Ecclesiastes," <u>F&SF</u>, 25 (November), 5-35.

    Avram Davidson, ed. <u>The Best from Fantasy and Science Fiction</u>. Garden City, N.Y.: Doubleday, 1965.
    Judith Merrill, ed. <u>The 10th Annual of the Year's Best S-F</u>. New York: Delacorte, 1965.
    In <u>Four for Tomorrow</u>, 1967.
    Robert Silverberg, ed. <u>The Science Fiction Hall of Fame</u>. Garden City, NY.: Doubleday, 1970.
    In <u>The Doors of His Face, The Lamps of His Mouth, and Other Stories</u>, 1971.
    Dick Allen, ed. <u>Science Fiction: The Future</u>. New York: Harcourt Brace Jovanovich, 1971 [paper].
    Stephen V. Shaley and Stanley J. Cook, eds. <u>Man Unwept: Visions From the Inner Eye</u>. New York: McGraw-Hill, 1974 [paper].
    Patricia Warrick and Martin Harry Greenberg, eds. <u>The New Awareness: Religion Through Science Fiction</u>. New York: Delacorte, 1975.
    Adaptation, <u>see</u> A112 and A113.

A25   "The Great Slow Kings," <u>Worlds of Tomorrow</u>, 1 (December), 97-102.

    Tom Boardman, Jr., ed. <u>An ABC of Science Fiction</u>. New York: Avon, 1968 [paper].
    Robert Hoskins, ed. <u>The Stars Around Us</u>. New York: New American Library, 1970 [paper].
    In <u>The Doors of His Face, The Lamps of His Mouth, and Other Stories</u>, 1971.

1964

A26 "The Graveyard Heart," Fantastic, 13 (March),
     20-71.

     In Four for Tomorrow, 1967.
     Robert Silverberg, ed. Great Short Novels of SF.
        New York: Ballantine, 1970 [paper].
     James Sallis, ed. The Shores Beneath. New York:
        Avon, 1971 [paper].

A27 "Collector's Fever," Galaxy, 22 (June), 129-131.

     In The Doors of His Face, The Lamps of His Mouth,
        and Other Stories, 1971.
     Adaptation, see A113.
     Isaac Asimov, Martin Harry Greenberg, and
        Joseph T. Olander, eds. 100 Great Science
        Fiction Short Short Stories. Garden City,
        N.Y.: Doubleday, 1978.

A28 "Lucifer," Worlds of Tomorrow, 2 (June), 81-85.

     In The Doors of His Face, The Lamps of His Mouth,
        and Other Stories, 1971.

A29 "The Salvation of Faust," F&SF, 27 (July), 76-79.

     Peter Haining, ed. The Black Magic Omnibus. New
        York: Taplinger, 1976.

A30 "The New Pleasure," Double:Bill [fanzine], no. 10
     (August), pp. 23-24.

A31 "The Night Has Nine Hundred Ninety-Nine Eyes,"
     Double:Bill [fanzine], no. 11 (October-November),
     pp. 15-16.

A32   "The Monster and the Maiden," <u>Galaxy</u>, 23 (December), 105.

        Frederick Pohl, ed. <u>The Ninth Galaxy Reader</u>.
           Garden City, N.Y.: Doubleday, 1966.
        In <u>The Doors of His Face, The Lamps of His Mouth,</u>
           <u>and Other Stories</u>, 1971.
        Robert Hoskins, ed. <u>Wondermakers 2</u>. New York:
           Fawcett, 1974 [paper].

1965

A33   "He Who Shapes," <u>Amazing</u>, 38, Part One (January), 72-112; Part Two (February), 51-90.

        Damon Knight, ed. <u>Nebula Award Stories: 1965</u>.
           Garden City, N.Y.: Doubleday, 1966.
        Expanded version as <u>The Dream Master</u>. New York:
           Ace, 1966 [paper].
        London: Rupert Hart-Davis, 1968 [first hardcover
           edition].
        London: Panther, 1968 [paper].
        Boston: Gregg Press, 1976 [first U.S. hardcover
           edition; photographic reproduction of the 1966
           Ace first printing].

A34   "Passage to Dilfar," <u>Fantastic</u>, 14 (February), 49-53.

      *<u>Sorcerer's Apprentice</u> (Winter 1979) [Source:
           Zelazny].

A35   "The Doors of His Face, The Lamps of His Mouth," <u>F&SF</u>, 28 (March), 4-30.

        Edward Ferman, ed. <u>The Best from Fantasy and
           Science Fiction: Fifteenth Series</u>. Garden
           City, N.Y.: Doubleday, 1966.

Damon Knight, ed. <u>Nebula Award Stories: 1965</u>.
   Garden City, N.Y.: 1966.
In <u>Four for Tomorrow</u>, 1967.
Edmund Crispin, ed. <u>Best SF 7</u>. London: Faber,
   1970.
In <u>The Doors of His Face, The Lamps of His Mouth,
   and Other Stories</u>, 1971.
Martin Harry Greenberg, Joseph D. Olander, and
   Patricia Warrick, eds. <u>Run to Starlight:
   Sports Through Science Fiction</u>. New York:
   Delacorte, 1975.
Adaptation, <u>see</u> A113.

A36   "Devil Car," <u>Galaxy</u>, 23 (June), 151-163.

Frederick Pohl, ed. <u>The Tenth Galaxy Reader</u>.
   Garden City, N.Y.: Doubleday, 1967.
In <u>The Doors of His Face, The Lamps of His Mouth,
   and Other Stories</u>, 1971.
Bernard Hollister, ed. <u>Another Tomorrow</u>. Day-
   ton, Ohio: Pflaum, 1974 [paper].
*<u>Science Fiction Scope Activity Kit</u>, 1976. [Stu-
   dent Booklet "written and compiled by the
   editors of <u>Scholastic Scope</u> Magazine,"
   according to Zelazny, who notes that this ver-
   sion is "excerpted, chopped, and channeled."]
Brian Aldiss and Harry Harrison, eds. <u>Decade:
   The 60s</u>. London: Macmillan, 1977.
Robert Silverberg, Martin Harry Greenberg, and
   Joseph D. Olander, eds. <u>Car Sinister</u>. New
   York: Avon, 1979 [paper].

A37   "The Furies," <u>Amazing</u>, 38 (June), 11-41.

In <u>Four for Tomorrow</u>, 1967.
<u>Thrilling SF</u> (October 1972).
Adaptation, <u>see</u> A113.

A38   "Of Time and Yan," <u>F&SF</u>, 28 (June), 110-112.

A39   "Thelinde's Song," <u>Fantastic</u>, 14 (June), 5-11.

<u>Strange Fantasy</u> (Fall 1970).
Lin Carter, ed. <u>Realms of Wizardry</u>. Garden
    City, N.Y.: Doubleday, 1976.

A40   ". . . And Call Me Conrad," <u>F&SF</u>, 29, Part One
(October), 5-57; Part Two (November), 39-97.

As <u>This Immortal</u>. New York: Ace, 1966 [paper].
London: Rupert Hart-Davis, 1967 [first hardcover
    edition].
London: Panther, 1968 [paper].
New York & London: Garland Publishing, 1975
    [first U.S. hardcover edition, photographic
    reproduction of the 1973 Ace third printing].

A41   "The Drawing," <u>Algol</u> [fanzine], no. 10 (September), pp. 15-16.

A42   "But Not the Herald," <u>Magazine of Horror</u>, no. 12
(Winter), pp. 33-35.

A43   "The Injured," <u>Kronos</u> [fanzine], no. 2 [undated;
internal references indicate 1965], pp. 12-13
[cf. table of contents; pages are unnumbered].

1966

A44   "Love is an Imaginary Number," <u>New Worlds</u>,
    no. 158 (January), pp. 86-92.

In <u>The Doors of His Face, The Lamps of His Mouth,
and Other Stories</u>, 1971.

A45   "The Bells of Shoredan," Fantastic, 15 (March),
       6-21.

       Hans Stefan Santesson, ed. Mighty Swordsmen.
          New York: Lancer, 1970 [paper].
       L. Sprague de Camp, ed. Warlocks and Warriors.
          New York: Berkley, 1971 [paper].
       Published as a separate pamphlet, Columbia, PA:
          Underwood/Miller, 1979.

A46   "For a Breath I Tarry," New Worlds, no. 160
       (March), pp. 91-128.

       Fantastic, 16 (September), 6-37. [The New Worlds
          text is garbled; Fantastic version is text for
          all subsequent reprints.]
       Donald A. Wolheim and Terry Carr, eds. The
          World's Best Science Fiction: 1967. New York:
          Ace, 1967 [paper].
       Michael Moorcock, ed. Best S.F. Stories from New
          Worlds 2. London: Panther, 1968 [paper].
       Alan Danzig, ed. The Theme of the Machine.
          Dubuque, Iowa: Wm. C. Brown, 1969 [paper].
       Robert Silverberg, ed. Alpha 1. New York:
          Ballantine, 1970 [paper].
       John S. Lambert, ed. The New Prometheans: Read-
          ings for the Future. New York: Harper & Row,
          1973 [paper].
       Total Effect, ed. Survival Printout. New York:
          Vintage, 1973 [paper].
       Norman Spinrad, ed. Modern Science Fiction. New
          York: Anchor, 1974 [paper].

A47   This Immortal. [No month of publication listed,
       but review in Yandro (fanzine), no. 160 (June)
       suggests May as probable date.] See A40.

A48   "This Moment of the Storm," <u>F&SF</u>, 30 (June),
      4-30.

      Edward L. Ferman, ed. <u>The Best from Fantasy and
          Science Fiction, Sixteenth Series</u>. Garden
          City, N.Y.: Doubleday, 1967.
      In <u>The Doors of His Face, The Lamps of His Mouth,
          and Other Stories</u>, 1971.
      Gardner R. Dozois, ed. <u>A Day in the Life</u>. New
          York: Harper & Row, 1972.

A49   "Divine Madness," <u>Magazine of Horror</u>, no. 13
      (Summer), pp. 30-35.

      <u>New Worlds</u>, no. 167 (October), pp. 98-104.
      Terry Carr, ed. <u>New Worlds of Fantasy</u>. New
          York: Ace, 1967 [paper].
      Michael Moorcock, ed. <u>The Traps of Time</u>. Lon-
          don: Rapp & Whiting, 1968.
      In <u>The Doors of His Face, The Lamps of His Mouth,
          and Other Stories</u>, 1971.

A50   <u>The Dream Master</u>. [No month of publication
      listed, but review in <u>Yandro</u> (fanzine), no. 163
      (September) suggests August as probable date.]
      <u>See</u> A33.

A51   "The Keys to December," New Worlds, no. 165
      (August), pp. 115-141.

      Michael Moorcock, ed. <u>The Best S.F. Stories from
          New Worlds</u>. London: Panther, 1967 [paper].
      Donald A. Wolheim and Terry Carr, eds. <u>The
          World's Best Science Fiction: 1967</u>. New
          York: Ace, 1967 [paper].
      In <u>The Doors of His Face, The Lamps of His Mouth,
          and Other Stories</u>, 1971.

A52   "The House of the Hanged Man," <u>Double:Bill</u> [fan-
      ine], no. 15 (September), pp. 10-12.

A53   "Comes Now the Power," <u>Magazine of Horror</u>, no. 14 (Winter), pp. 55-60.

      *Lee Harding, ed. <u>Beyond Tomorrow</u>. South Melbourne, Australia: Wren, 1976. [Source: Zelazny.]

1967

A54   <u>Four for Tomorrow</u>. Introduction by Theodore Sturgeon. New York: Ace [paper]. [No month of publication listed, but review in <u>Yandro</u> (fanzine), no. 168 (February) suggests January as probable date.] [Contents: "The Furies," 1965; "The Graveyard Heart," 1964; "The Doors of His Face, The Lamps of His Mouth," 1965; "A Rose for Ecclesiastes," 1963.]

      London: Rupert Hart-Davis, 1969, as <u>A Rose for Ecclesiastes</u> [first hardcover edition].
      London: Panther, 1969, as <u>A Rose for Ecclesiastes</u> [paper].
      New York & London: Garland Publishing, 1975 [first U.S. hardcover edition; photographic reproduction of the 1973 Ace second printing].

A55   "This Mortal Mountain," <u>If</u>, 17 (March), 37-67.

      In <u>The Doors of His Face, The Lamps of His Mouth, and Other Stories</u>, 1971.
      Terry Carr, ed. <u>This Side of Infinity</u>. New York: Ace, 1972 [paper].

A56   "Dawn," <u>F&SF</u>, 32 (April), 4-35.

      Chapter ii of <u>Lord of Light</u> (<u>see</u> A63).

A57 "Death and the Executioner," F&SF, 32 (June), 4-36.

   Chapter iii of Lord of Light. See A63.

A58 "The Man Who Loved the Faioli," Galaxy, 25 (June), pp. 67-73.

   Donald A. Wolheim and Terry Car, eds. The World's Best Science Fiction: 1968. New York: Ace, 1968 [paper].
   In The Doors of His Face, The Lamps of His Mouth, and Other Stories, 1971.
   Harry Harrison, ed. SF: Author's Choice 4. New York: Putnam, 1974.

A59 "In the House of the Dead," New Worlds, no. 173 (July), pp. 51-59.

   Excerpt from Creatures of Light and Darkness. See A80.

A60 "Angel, Dark Angel," Galaxy, 25 (August), 57-67.

   Robert Hoskins, ed. Far-Out People. New York: New American Library, 1971 [paper].

*A61 "Pattern in Rebma," Kallikanzaros [fanzine], no. 1 [no information available on date, but logically must have appeared before A62].

   [Reading, transcribed, from Nine Princes in Amber--Source: Zelazny.]

A62 "A Knight for Merytha," Kallikanzaros [fanzine], no. 2 (September), pp. 7-12. [Part of the Dilvish series; not submitted to Fantastic because of change in editor and owner.]

Procrastination [fanzine], no. 9 (n.d.).
Eternity [fanzine], no. 3 (1964).
*Eternity, 1 (1979). [Source: Zelazny.]

A63   Lord of Light. Garden City, N.Y.: Doubleday
[publication date: September 22]. See A56 and
A57.

Garden City, N.Y.: Doubleday, 1968. [Science
    Fiction Book Club edition]
London: Faber and Faber, 1968.
New York: Avon, 1969 [paper].
London: Panther, 1971 [paper].
Boston: Gregg Press, 1979. [Photographic repro-
    duction of the 1967 Doubleday edition.]

A64   "Auto-da-fe," Dangerous Visions, Harlan Ellison,
ed. Garden City, N.Y.: Doubleday [publication
date: 20 October, pp. 500-506.

Rob Sauer, ed. Voyages: Scenarios for a Ship
    Called Earth. Ballantine, 1971 [paper].   ·
Leo P. Kelley, ed. Fantasy: The Literature of
    the Marvelous. New York: McGraw-Hill, 1974
    [paper].

A65   "Damnation Alley," Galaxy, 26 (October), 6-83.

Considerably expanded as Damnation Alley. New
    York: Putnam, 1969.
New York: Berkley, 1970 [paper].
London: Faber & Faber, 1971.
London: Sphere, 1973 [paper].
New York: Berkley, 1977 [paper; movie tie-in
    edition with stills from the film].
Boston: Gregg Press, 1979. [Includes stills
    from the film; photographic reproduction from
    the 1969 Putnam edition].

A66   "The Last Inn on the Road" [collaboration with
      Danny Plachta], New Worlds, no. 176 (October),
      pp. 55-57.

      Michael Moorcock, ed. Best S.F. Stories from New
         Worlds 5. London: Panther, 1969 [paper].

*A67 "A Hand Across the Galaxy," Arioch [fanzine],
      no. 1 (November), pp. 14-15. [Source: Zelazny.]

A68   "The Princes," Kallikanzaros [fanzine], no. 3
      (December 1967-January 1968), pp. 5-10. [Sub-
      titled "An Excerpt from Nine Princes in Amber, A
      Novel-in-Progress"; especially notable for ten
      illustrations by Jack Gaughan, showing the nine
      princes and the unicorn on their respective trump
      cards (unicorn's trump used as the fanzine's
      cover).]

1968

A69   "He That Moves," If, 18 (January), 153-159.

A70   "Dismal Light," If, 18 (May), 60-71.

A71   "Stowaway," Odd [fanzine], no. 19 (Summer),
      pp. 12-13.

      Mentat [fanzine], no. 11 (May 1969).

A72   "Song of the Blue Baboon," If, 18 (August), 91-94.

A73   "Creatures of Light," If, 18 (November), 68-98,
      153-157.

      Excerpt from Creatures of Light and Darkness
         (A80).

A74 "Corrida," Anubis [semi-prozine], no. 3 (n.d.),
pp. 5-6.

In The Doors of His Face, The Lamps of His Mouth,
and Other Stories, 1971.
Isaac Asimov, Martin Harry Greenberg, and
Joseph D. Olander, eds. 100 Great Science
Fiction Short Short Stories. Garden City,
N.Y.: Doubleday, 1978.

A75 Nebula Award Stories Three [anthology]. Garden
City, N.Y.: Doubleday. [No month of publication listed.]

London: Victor Gollancz, 1968.
New York: Pocket Books, 1970 [paper].
London: Panther, 1970 [paper].

1969

A76 "The Steel General," If, 19 (January), 68-98,
156-158. Excerpt from Creatures of Light and
Darkness. See A80.

A77 Isle of the Dead. New York: Ace, 1969 [paper].
[No month of publication listed, but review in
Yandro (fanzine), no. 186 (March) suggests
February is probable date.]

London: Rapp and Whiting, 1970 [first hardcover
edition].
Boston: Gregg Press, 1976 [first U.S. hardcover
edition; photographic reproduction of the 1969
Ace first printing].

A78 "Creatures of Darkness," If, 19 (March), 139-158.
Excerpt from Creatures of Light and Darkness.
See A80.

A79   A Rose for Ecclesiastes. [British edition of
        Four for Tomorrow; hardcover published in June,
        paperback in November.] See A54.

A80   Creatures of Light and Darkness. Garden City,
        N.Y.: Doubleday [publication date: Septem-
        ber 12]. See A59, A72, A75, and A77.

        New York: Avon, 1970 [paper].
        London: Faber and Faber, 1970.
        London: Arrow, 1972 [paper].

A81   "Come to Me Not in Winter's White" [collaboration
        with Harlan Ellison], F&SF, 37 (October), 24-33.

        Knight, 7 (December 1969).
        Harlan Ellison, ed. Partners in Wonder. New
          York: Walker, 1971.

A82   Damnation Alley. [Published in October.]
        See A65.

A83   "The Year of the Good Seed" [collaboration with
        Dannie Plachta], Galaxy, 29 (December), 85-89.

A84   "The Eve of RUMOKO," in Three for Tomorrow [anon-
        ymously ed. by Robert Silverberg]. New York:
        Meredith [no month of publication listed],
        pp. 85-152.

        In My Name is Legion, 1976.

*A85   "Heritage," Cetacean [Baltimore advertising maga-
        zine, no. 6 (n.d.), pp. 7, 21. [Source:
        Zelazny.]

1970

A86 "My Lady of the Diodes," <u>Granfaloon</u> [fanzine],
no. 8 (January), pp. 27-37, 49-54.

A87 <u>Nine Princes in Amber</u>. Garden City, N.Y.:
Doubleday [publication date: 26 June]. <u>See</u> A61
and A68.

 New York: Avon, 1972 [paper].
 London: Faber and Faber, 1972.
 London: Corgi, 1974 [paper].
 *Bloomington, IN: John Onoda, 1975. [The first
  half of the novel adapted to comic-book format;
  source, Zelazny.]
 Boston: Gregg Press, 1979. [Photographic repro-
  duction of the 1970 Doubleday edition.]
 In <u>The Chronicles of Amber</u>, 1979.

*A88 "The Man at the Corner of Now and Forever,"
<u>Exile</u> [fanzine], no. 7 (n.d.), pp 6-15. [Source:
Zelazny]

1971

A89 <u>The Doors of His Face, The Lamps of His Mouth,
and Other Stories</u>. Garden City, N.Y.: Doubleday
[publication date: 18 June]. [Contents: "The
Doors of His Face, The Lamps of His Mouth," 1965;
"The Keys to December," 1966; "Devil Car," 1965;
"A Rose for Ecclesiastes," 1963; "The Monster and
the Maiden," 1964; "Collector's Fever," 1964;
"This Mortal Mountain," 1967; "This Moment of the
Storm," 1966; "The Great Slow Kings," 1963; "A
Museum Piece," 1963; "Divine Madness," 1966;
"Corrida," 1968; "Love is an Imaginary Number,"
1966; "The Man Who Loved the Faioli," 1967;
"Lucifer," 1964.]

London: Faber and Faber, 1973.
New York: Avon, 1974 [paper].
London: Corgi, 1975 [paper].

A90 "Jack of Shadows," F&SF, 41, Part One (July),
5-59; Part Two (August), 16-62.

Jack of Shadows. New York: Walker, 1971.
New York: Walker, 1971? [Science Fiction Book
    Club Edition].
New York: New American Library, 1972 [paper].
London: Faber and Faber, 1973. [Copyright page
    bears the statement "First published in 1972,"
    but the official publication date was 8 Janu-
    ary 1973.]
London: Corgi, 1974 [paper].

A91 Jack of Shadows. See A89.

1972

A92 The Guns of Avalon. Garden City, N.Y.: Doubleday [publication date: 27 October].

London: Faber and Faber, 1974.
New York: Avon, 1974 [paper].
London: Corgi, 1975 [paper].
In The Chronicles of Amber, 1979.

1973

A93 Today We Choose Faces. New York: New American
Library [publication date: 1 April] [paper].

London: Millington, 1974 [first hardcover edi-
    tion].
London: Orbit, 1976 [paper].

Boston: Gregg Press, 1979 [first U.S. hardcover edition; photographic reproduction of the 1973 New American Library edition].

A94 <u>To Die in Italbar</u>. Garden City, N.Y.: Doubleday [publication date: 13 July].

Garden City, N.Y.: Doubleday, 1973. [Science Fiction Book Club edition.]
New York: DAW, 1974 [paper].
London: Faber and Faber, 1975.
London: Corgi, 1977 [paper].

A95 "'Kjwalll'kje'k'koothaïlll'kje'k," <u>An Exaltation of Stars: Transcendental Adventures in Science Fiction</u>, ed. Terry Carr. New York: Simon and Schuster [no publication date listed], pp. 71-140.

In <u>My Name is Legion</u>, 1976.

1974

A96 "The Engine at Heartspring's Center," <u>Analog</u>, 93 (July), 70-76.

Terry Carr, ed. <u>Best SF of the Year #4</u>. New York: Ballantine, 1975 [paper].
James Gunn, ed. <u>Nebula Award Stories Ten</u>. New York: Harper & Row, 1975.

1975

A97 "Sign of the Unicorn," <u>Galaxy</u>, 36, Part One (January), 15-64; Part Two (February), 105-146; Part Three (March), 82-112.

<u>Sign of the Unicorn</u>. Garden City, N.Y.: Double-day [publication date: 21 February].

New York: Avon, 1976 [paper].
London: Faber and Faber, 1977.
London: Corgi, 1978 [paper].
In The Chronicles of Amber, 1979.

A98   Sign of the Unicorn. See A97.

A99   "The Game of Blood and Dust," Galaxy, 36 (April),
       5-8.

       James Baen, ed. The Best from Galaxy, Volume IV.
           New York: Award, 1976 [paper].
       Patricia Warrick, Martin Harry Greenberg, and
           Joseph Olander, eds. Science Fiction: Con-
           temporary Mythology. New York: Harper & Row,
           1978.

A100   "Doorways in the Sand," Analog, 95, Part One
       (June), 12-64; Part Two (July), 68-109; Part
       Three (August), 78-131.

       Doorways in the Sand. New York: Harper & Row,
           1976 [publication date: 31 March].
       New York: Harper & Row, 1976 [Science Fiction
           Book Club Edition].
       New York: Avon, 1977 [paper].
       London: W. H. Allen, 1977.
       London: Star, 1978 [paper].

A101   "Home is the Hangman," Analog, 95 (November),
       14-66.

       In My Name is Legion, 1976.
       Ursula K. Le Guin, ed. Nebula Award Stories 11.
           London: Gollancz, 1976.
       Ben Bova, ed. The Best of Analog. New York:
           Baronet, 1978 [trade paperback].

1976

A102   Doorways in the Sand. See A100.

A103   My Name is Legion. New York: Ballantine [publica-
        tion date: April] [paper]. [Contents: "The Eve
        of RUMOKO," 1969; "'Kjwalll'kje'k'koothaïlll'kje'k,"
        1973; "Home is the Hangman," 1975.]

        London: Faber and Faber, 1979 [first hardcover
            edition].

A104   "The Hand of Oberon," Galaxy, 37, Part One (May),
        8-51; Part Two (July), 45-95; Part Three (Septem-
        ber), 86-107.

        The Hand of Oberon. Garden City, N.Y.: Double-
            day [publication date: June].
        New York: Avon, 1977 [paper].
        London: Faber and Faber, 1978.
        London: Sphere, 1979 [paper].
        In The Chronicles of Amber, 1979.

A105   The Hand of Oberon. See A106.

A106   Bridge of Ashes. New York: New American Library
        [publication date: July] [paper].

        Boston: Gregg Press, 1979 [first hardcover edi-
            tion; photographic reproduction of the 1976
            New American Library first printing].

A107   Deus Irae [collaboration with Philip K. Dick].
        Garden City, N.Y.: Doubleday [publication date:
        20 August].

        New York: Dell, 1977 [paper].
        London: Victor Gollancz, 1977.
        London: Sphere, 1978 [paper].

A108   "The Force That Through the Circuit Drives the Current," <u>Science Fiction Discoveries</u>, ed. Carol and Frederick Pohl. New York: Bantam [publication date: August] [paper], pp. 123–129.

1977

A109   "No Award," <u>The Saturday Evening Post</u>, 249 (February), <u>57</u>, 93–95.

A110   "Is There a Demon Lover in the House," <u>Heavy Metal</u>, 1 (September), 43–44.

A111   "The Courts of Chaos," <u>Galaxy</u>, Part One, 38 (November), 5–41; Part Two, 39 (December–January 1978), 65–105; Part Three (February), 99–132.

        <u>The Courts of Chaos</u>. Garden City, N.Y.: 1978 [publication date: 6 October].
New York: Avon, 1979 [paper].
In <u>The Chronicles of Amber</u>, 1979.

1978

A112   "A Rose for Ecclesiastes," <u>Heavy Metal</u>, 1 (January), 77–96. [Rather than a reprint, this is Zelazny's <u>adaptation</u> of the story for comic-book format; art by Gray Morrow.]

        In <u>The Illustrated Roger Zelazny</u>, 1978.

A113   <u>The Illustrated Roger Zelazny</u> [illustrated by Gray Morrow]. New York: Baronet. [Simultaneous issue of copies in hardcover (2500 copies with tipped in limitation leaf signed by Zelazny and illustrator Morrow) and trade paper.] [Publication date: February.] [Contents: "Shadowjack" (prequel to <u>Jack of Shadows</u>); "An Amber Tapestry"

25

(mural of characters from the Amber novels); "A
Rose for Ecclesiastes," original version 1963 but
this is Zelazny-approved abridgment (see A112);
"The Furies," original version 1965, another
adaptation; "A Zelazny Tapestry" (characters and
scenes from Today We Choose Faces, Doorways in
the Sand, and Damnation Alley); "The Doors of His
Face, The Lamps of His Mouth," original version
1965; "Rock Collector," ("Collector's Fever),
original version 1964 (includes brief personal
comments by Zelazny and Morrow, as well as brief
commentary by Zelazny with all adapted stories).]

New York: Baronet, 1978. [Science Fiction Book
Club edition.]
New York: Ace, 1979 [mass market paper; re-
designed for smaller format, omits Zelazny's
personal statement but adds brief commentary
on the Amber characters, "An Amber Tapestry"
broken down into smaller panels].

A114 The Courts of Chaos. See A111.

A115 "Stand Pat, Ruby Stone," Destinies ["paperback
magazine"], ed. James Baen. New York: Ace
[Volume 1; publication date: November-December.]
[paper], pp. 4-16.

1979

A116 The Chronicles of Amber. Garden City, N.Y.:
Nelson Doubleday [issued by Doubleday for the
Science Fiction Book Club]. Two vols. [Publica-
tion date: January.] [Contents: Nine Princes
in Amber, 1970; The Guns of Avalon, 1972; Sign of
the Unicorn, 1975; The Hand of Oberson, 1976; The
Courts of Chaos, 1977-1978 (text is reset, but
without authorial revision).]

A117   <u>The Bells of Shoredan</u>. [Publication date: May.]
<u>See</u> A45.

A118   "Halfjack," <u>Omni</u>, 1 (June), 67-68.

*A119   "Garden of Blood," <u>Sorcerer's Apprentice</u>, no. 3
(Summer), pp. 16-20. [Source: Zelazny.]

A120   "The Last Defender of Camelot," <u>Asimov's SF Adventure Magazine</u>, 1 (Summer), 12-22.

A121   "The White Beast," <u>Whispers</u>, 4 (October), 116-118.

A122   "Go Starless in the Night," <u>Destinies</u> ["paperback
magazine"], ed. James Baen. New York: Ace
[Volume 1; publication date: October-December.]
[paper], pp. 8-19.

A123   <u>Roadmarks</u>. New York: Del Ray/Ballantine [publi-
cation date: October].

A124   "A Very Good Year," <u>Harvey</u>, 1 (December), 40, 90.

Unlocated fiction: "I did have some stuff published in
fanzines in the early 50s, but I no longer have
copies and my memory fails me totally"--Zelazny.

Also, Zelazny's interview in the fanzine <u>Mentat</u>
(C23) states that an excerpt from <u>Creatures of Light
and Darkness</u> was published under the title "At the
Carnival of Life" in <u>Stellar Stories of Imagination</u>.
Zelazny has no further information. The magazine
probably was Ted White's attempt to launch a professional magazine in 1968 (cf. his letter in <u>Locus</u>
[fanzine], no. 226 [October 1979], p. 16).

Part B: Poetry

1954

B1   "Diet," <u>Eucuyo</u> [Euclid High School literary maga-
      zine], p. 34.

      *<u>Young America Sings</u>. Los Angeles: National High
         School Poetry Association, 1954. [Source:
         Zelazny.]

1955

B2   "Slush, Slush, Slush," <u>Eucuyo</u> [Euclid High·School
      literary magazine], p. 10.

1958

B3   "The Man Without a Shadow," <u>Skyline</u> [Western
      Reserve University literary magazine], 31 (April),
      pp. 21-23.

      <u>Amra</u> [fanzine], no. 34 (May 1965), pp. 12-13.
         [Identical to <u>Skyline</u> version except for addi-
         tion of brief opening quote from Dante's
         <u>Purgatorio</u>.]
      In <u>Poems</u>, 1974.

Part B: Poetry

1959

B4 "Decade Plus One of Rose," Skyline [Western Reserve University literary magazine], 32 (April), 30-31.

B5 "Tryptich," Skyline [Western Reserve University literary magazine], 32 (April), 44.

1964

B6 "Old Ohio Folkfrag," Double:Bill [fanzine], no. 9 (June), p. 9.

B7 "Somewhere a Piece of Colored Light," Double:Bill [fanzine], no. 10 (August), p. 29.

  In Poems, 1974.

B8 "Concert," Double:Bill [fanzine], no. 11 (October-November), p. 32.

B9 "Song of the Ring," Niekas [fanzine], no. 10 (December 15), p. 10.

1965

*B10 "I, a Stranger and Revisited," Mercenary [fanzine] (Spring). [Source: Zelazny.]

B11 "The Man Without a Shadow." See B3.

B12 "Lamentation of the Prematurely Old Satyr," Yandro [fanzine], no. 149 (July), p. 9.

*B13 "On the Return of the Mercurian Flamebird After Nesting," Mercenary [fanzine] (Summer). [Source: Zelazny.]

B14 "Testament," <u>Kronos</u> [fanzine], no. 2 (n.d.) [p. 27]. [Date of 1965 conjectured from internal references; pages unnumbered.]

1966

B15 "Cross Caribbean," <u>Eridanus</u> [fanzine], no. 2 (June), p. 13. [Page number by count; pages un-numbered, printed on one side only.] <u>See</u> C6.

In <u>Poems</u>, 1974.

B16 "Day of Doom," <u>Niekas</u> [fanzine], no. 16 (June), p. 58.

B17 "Brahman Trimurti," <u>Nyarlathotep</u> [fanzine], no. 3 (July), p. 26.

In <u>Poems</u>, 1974.

B18 "Lamentations of the Venusian Pensioner, Golden Apples of the Sun Retirement Home, Earthcolony VI, Pdeth, Venus," <u>Double:Bill</u> [fanzine], no. 15 (September), p. 31.

1967

B19 "What Is [sic] Left When the Soul is Sold," <u>Yandro</u> [fanzine], no. 166 [January], p. 12.

B20 "Pyramid," <u>Infinite Fanac</u> [fanzine], no. 9 (August), p. 11.

B21 "The Cat Licks Her Coat," <u>Tapeworm</u> [fanzine], no. 5 (n.d.), p. 6. [Date of 1967 conjectured from strong internal evidence.]

1968

*B22 "Morning With Music," Trypod [fanzine], no. 2
   (March). [Source: Zelazny.]

   Eternity Science Fiction [fanzine], no. 1
   (July 1972).

B23 "There is Always a Poem," Double:Bill [fanzine],
   no. 18 (March-April), p. 15.

B24 "Thoughts of the Jupiterian Frantifier Fish During
   the 'Night' Freeze At [sic] Which Time, Unfortunately, Consciousness is Maintained by the Fish,
   Who are, Also Unfortunately, Quite Intelligent and
   Highly Sensitive Creatures--Alas!," Kallikanzaros
   [fanzine], no. 4 (March-April), pp. 24-25.

   In Poems, 1974.

*B25 "Diadonnenos of Polycletus," Haunted: Studies in
   Gothic Fiction, 1 (June), 77. [Source: Zelazny.]

*B26 "St. Secaires," Haunted: Studies in Gothic Fic-
   tion, 1 (June), 78. [Souce: Zelazny.]

B27 "Dim," Sirruish [fanzine], no. 7 (July), p. 42.

B28 "Moonsong," Sirruish [fanzine], no. 7 (July),
   p. 41.

   Procrastination [fanzine], no. 10 [n.d.; 1972 by
    internal evidence.

1974

B29 Poems. Discon [published in 1,000 copy edition
   for the first 1,000 members of the Discon] [pa-
   per]. Illustrated by Jack Gaughan. [Contents:
   "Braxa" (from "A Rose for Ecclesiastes"), 1963;

"Brahman Trimurti," 1966; "Thoughts of the
Jupiterian Frantifier Fish . . . ," 1968; "Future,
Be Not Impatient" from "The Graveyard Heart"),
1964; "Somewhere a Piece of Colored Light," 1964;
"Southern Cross (Elegy, Hart Crane)" (retitled
"Cross Caribbean"), 1966; "The De-Synonymization
of Winter," no source or date listed; "Flight"
(from "The Graveyard Heart"), 1964; "What is Left
When the Soul is Sold," 1967; "Our Wintered Way
Through Evening, and Burning Bushes Along It"
(from "The Graveyard Heart"), 1964; "The Man
Without a Shadow," 1965 (see B3); "In the Dogged
House" (from "The Graveyard Heart"), 1964.]

1977

B30   "I, The Crooked Rose's Dream, Dumb-Sung Anatomie,"
The Speculative Poetry Review [fanzine], no. 2
(n.d.], n.p.

B31   "Faust Before Twelve," The Speculative Poetry Review [fanzine], 7 (n.d.), 39.

B32   "Wriggle Under George Washington Bridge," The
Speculative Poetry Review [fanzine], 7 (n.d.), 38.

1978

B33   "Dark Horse Shadow," Ariel: The Book of Fantasy,
3 (April), 64. [Both this and B34 are excerpts
from Creatures of Light and Darkness (A80),
printed here as poems.]

B34   "Thundershoon," Ariel: The Book of Fantasy, 3
(April), 67. See B33.

B35   "Ducks," T.A.ofS.P. [The Anthology of Speculative
Poetry]]fanzine], no. 3 (n.d.), 28.

Part C: Nonfiction

Items in less available and/or likely sources have been annotated.

C1   "Two Traditions and Cyril Tourneur: An Examination of Morality and Humor Comedy Conventions in 'The Revenger's Tragedy.'" M.A. thesis, Columbia University.

      Connection to Zelazny's own work is somewhat remote. However, Tourneur's play was the direct model of an early (and Zelazny-disowned) story, "Nine Starships Waiting" (A13), and Zelazny's comment that "a universe denuded of spiritual significance may be horrible--it may also be a comic universe" (p. 44) may prefigure the tone of some later works, especially Creatures of Light and Darkness (A80).

C2   "Editorial," Amazing, 36 (December), 128.

      To satisfy reader curiosity about Zelazny, editor Cele Goldsmith quotes three paragraphs by Zelazny describing his background and tastes.

1963

C3   "D:B Symposium" [questionnaire for professional science fiction writers and editors], Double:Bill [fanzine], no. 7 (October), pp. 78-79, 81, 84-85, 88, 90, 92, 94, 98. [Pages noted are those containing Zelazny's replies.]

The Double:Bill Symposium. Akron, Ohio: D:B Press, 1969 [publication date: September] [paper].

*C4 "Sundry Notes on Dybology and Suchlike," Science Fiction Parade [fanzine], 36 (September), 2-5. [Source: Zelazny. Bruce Pelz identifies fanzine as Half Life (ed. Stan Woolston). All other information identical.]
Comments on elements of "sfantasy," stressing people above everything else. Human attitudes shape interpretation of technology, and Zelazny says, "I now attempt to conceptualize my stories via character rather than gimmicks."

1965

C5 Letter to the Editor, Shangri L'Affairs [fanzine], no. 71 (July), p. 34.
Brief note accompanying resubscription, mentioning amusing anecdote about publishing puffery in edition of Sermon on the Mount.

1966

C6 Letter to the Editor, Eridanus [fanzine], no. 2 (Spring), [p. 16].
Says that "Cross Caribbean" won "Western Reserve University's Finlay Foster Poetry Prize in 1957, but was never published anywhere."

C7 "The Search for the Historical L. Sprague de Camp or, The Compleat Dragon-Catcher," Tricon Progress Report, no. 1 (n.d.), pp. 3-4.
Brief appreciation, survey of de Camp's work.

1967

C8   "De Gustibus," Nyarlathotep [fanzine], no. 5
      (May), pp. 44-46.
          Apparently in response to a review of This
      Immortal, written by Alexei Panshin and published
      in previous issue of Nyarlathotep. Graceful hom-
      age to Panshin and the importance of critics
      without ever getting into substance of review or
      the book.

C9   "On Writing and Stories," Science Fiction Times
      [fanzine], no. 446 ([September]), pp. 5-6.
          "Guest Editorial" on difference between in-
      spiration and craft in writing.

C10   "Afterward" to "Auto-da-fe," in Dangerous Visions,
      ed. Harlan Ellison. Garden City, N.Y.: Double-
      day, pp. 506-507 [publication date: 20 October].

C11   Letter to the Editor, Genook [fanzine], no. 3
      (October-November), p. 20.
          Brief acknowledgement of earlier issue.

C12   "Foreword: In Praise of His Spirits, Noble and
      Otherwise," in From the Land of Fear by Harlan
      Ellison. New York: Belmont [publication date:
      December] [paper], pp. 7-10.

C13   "Shadows," Kallikanzaros [fanzine], no. 3
      (December 1967-January 1968), pp. 11-16.
          Transcription of Zelazny's Guest of Honor
      Speech at the Detroit Triple Fan Fair, 1967.
      Speech itself takes up three and a half pages,
      followed by transcription of the question-and-
      answer period. Zelazny distinguishes sf from
      other popular genres by its tradition of fan ac-
      tivity. He compares literature to other media in
      use of shadows--the areas between what is actually
      shown (the panels of a comic strip, for example),

in which the imagination is free to operate; sf especially encourages imagination.

C14   "The Guest of Honor Speech, Ozarkon 2," <u>Sirruish</u> [fanzine], no. 5 (n.d.), pp. 37-43.
    Surveys history of literature to define Comedy and Tragedy, then uses Northrup Frye to insist that sf deals with High Mimetic characters, thus is more capable of real Comedy and Tragedy than "mainstream" literature. Uses <u>More than Human</u> (Sturgeon) and <u>Childhood's End</u> (Clarke) as examples.

C15   Letter to the Editor, <u>Tapeworm</u> [fanzine], no. 5 (n.d.--1967 conjectural), p. 23.

1968

C16   "Introduction" to <u>A Private Cosmos</u> by Philip José-Farmer. New York: Ace [paper], pp. v-ix. [No month of publication listed, but review in. <u>Yandro</u> (fanzine), #182 (July) suggests June as probable date.]

C17   Letter to the Editor, <u>Kallikanzaros</u> [fanzine], no. 5 (June-July), p. 56.
    Comment and addenda to Sandra Miesel's essay. See D42.

C18   "Re: A Rose for Ecclesiastes" [letter], <u>No-Eyed Monster</u> [fanzine], no. 14 (Summer), pp. 21-22.
    Unusually personal letter, linking self to Gallenger in "A Rose for Ecclesiastes."

C19   "Cordwainer Smith," <u>Riverside Quarterly</u> [fanzine], 3 (August), 232-233.
    Brief appreciation of Smith's work, expression of regret that Zelazny never overcame reserve to contact Smith and tell him how good he was.

C20   "Introduction" to <u>Nebula Award Stories Three</u>.
       Garden City, N.Y.: Doubleday, pp. ix–xi. [No
       publication month listed.]
           Zelazny also contributed headnotes for each
       story and also an afterword.

C21   <u>Secretary-Treasurer's Handbook: Science Fiction</u>
       <u>Writers of America</u>. n.p.
           Copy at Syracuse University is Xeroxed,
       punched (and reinforced) to fit a three-hole
       binder. Body is 15 pages of text by Zelazny;
       rest are appendixes (B36–37, and C39–41 also by
       Zelazny). Copies were "simply passed along by me
       to a few officers and officers-elect and other
       interested parties in the organization . . . with
       the balance given to Anne McCaffrey, my succes-
       sor"--Zelazny.

                         1969

C22   "Authorgraphs--An Interview with Roger Zelazny,"
       <u>If</u>, 19 (January), 159–161.

C23   "An Interview with Roger Zelazny" [conducted by
       editor Ulf Westblom], <u>Mentat</u> [fanzine], no. 11
       (May), pp. 200–203.
           Survey of career and opinions.

C24   <u>The Double:Bill Symposium</u>. [Publication date:
       September.] <u>See</u> C3.

                         1970

C25   "How About This? Roger Zelazny," <u>Phantasmicom</u>
       [fanzine], no. 2 (Winter), pp. 9–16.
           Transcript of radio interview conducted by
       Patrick Kelly, 13 December 1969. Discusses radio
       sf, Zelazny's own writing projects, and conclu-
       sion of <u>Creatures of Light and Darkness</u>.

1971

C26 "How About This? Roger Zelazny," <u>Phantasmicom</u>
[fanzine], no. 5 (April), pp. 11-14.
Transcript of (unbroadcast) radio interview
conducted by Patrick Kelly, July 1970. Discusses Zelazny's current writing projects (including his desire to do biographies) and past
career (including selling of "For a Breath I
Tarry").

C27 "Science Fiction and How it Got That Way," <u>The
Writer</u>, 84 (May), 15-17.

C28 Letter to the Editor. <u>Rats</u> [fanzine], no. 8
(June), p. 2.
Brief comment on selling "Auto da Fe" to
Ellison for <u>Dangerous Visions</u>.

C29 Dustjacket of <u>The Doors of His Face, The Lamps of
His Mouth, and Other Stories</u>. [Publication date:
18 June.] <u>See</u> A89.
Back quotes three paragraphs of personal background by Zelazny, actually written as autobio-
graphical sketch for <u>The Sun</u> (Baltimore),
21 January 1967 (in Roger Zelazny collection,
George Arents Research Library at Syracuse
University).

*C30 "Lester Del Rey: Toward a Sufficient Demonola-
try," <u>Marcon VI Program Booklet</u> [n.d.], pp. [3-4].
[Source: Zelazny.]

1972

C31 "Zelazny at Marcon '72," <u>Cosine</u> [fanzine], no. 3
(March 30), unpaged [2 pp.].
Summary of Zelazny's speech, with many brief
quotations, prepared by Bill Conner. Includes

comments on "A Rose for Ecclesiastes," Lord of
Light, Isle of the Dead, and Creatures of Light
and Darkness.

C32   "Rencontre avec Roger Zelazny" [interview conducted by Patrick Noel], Galaxy, no. 96 (May),
pp. 124-131.
    In French. Actual interview, pp. 126-128,
concerns Zelazny's opinions on New Wave sf, relationship between sf and literature, and other issues. Interpretive comments by interviewer.
Page 131 contains bibliography of Zelazny's work
published in French, both short stories (in
Galaxie and Fiction) and novels.

*C33   "A Brief Interview with Roger Zelazny," Nova
[fanzine], (June) pp. 33-35. [Source: Zelazny.]

C34   "Up Against the Wall, Roger Zelazny" [interview
conducted by Jeffrey D. Smith], Phantasmicom
[fanzine], no. 10 (November), pp. 14-18.

    The Alien Critic [fanzine], no. 7 (November 1973),
pp. 35-40, with additional questions by Richard E.
Geis.

C35   "An Interview with Roger Zelazny," Luna Monthly
[fanzine], no. 43 (December), pp. 1-3.

    Paul Walker. Speaking of Science Fiction. New
    York: LUNA Publications, 1978.
    Suggested by Paul Walker, but written entirely
by Zelazny in form of self interrogation.

1973

C36   "Author's Choice," Vector [fanzine], no. 65 (May-
June), pp. 42-44.

The Alien Critic [fanzine], no. 7 (November 1973), pp. 40-43.
   Zelazny's own discussion of intent and personal assessment of each of his novels: This Immortal, The Dream Master, Lord of Light, Isle of the Dead, Creatures of Light and Darkness, Damnation Alley, and Jack of Shadows. Reprint includes Zelazny's comments on Today We Choose Faces, published after the piece was written for Vector.

C37   "The Genre: A Geological Survey," The Sun (Baltimore), 24 June, p. D5.

Phantasmicom [fanzine], no. 11 (May 1974), pp. 55-57, with C38 and C39 under joint title "Three Newspaper Pieces."

*C38   "A Sense of Wonder," The Sun (Baltimore), 2 September.

Review of Rendezvous with Rama (Clarke); praise with a few faint damns.

Phantasmicom [fanzine], no. 11 (May 1974), pp. 57-58. See C37.

*C39   "Who Done it? And Why?," The Sun (Baltimore), 14 October.

Phantasmicom [fanzine], no. 11 (May 1974), pp. 58-59. See C37.

C40   Letter to the Editor, The Alien Critic [fanzine], no. 7 (November), p. 43.

Part C: Nonfiction

1974

C41 "Roger Zelazny Interviews Frederik Pohl," *Thrust Science Fiction* [fanzine], 2 (January), 3-6.

C42 "Three Newspaper Pieces." *See* C37.

C43 Introduction to "The Man Who Loved the Faioli," in *SF: Author's Choice 4*, ed. Harry Harrison. New York: Putnam, pp. 239-241. [No month of publication listed.]

1975

C44 "Some Science Fiction Parameters: A Biased View," *Galaxy*, 36 (July), 6-11.

Antaeus, 26-26 (Spring-Summer 1977).

C45 "Introduction" to *Philip K. Dick: Electric Shepherd*, ed. Bruce Gillespie (Best of *SF Commentary* Number 1). Melbourne, Australia: Norstrilla Press, pp. 3-4. [No month of publication listed.]

1976

C46 "Ideas, Digressions and Daydreams: The Amazing Science Fiction Machine," *Insight* [Case Western Reserve University alumni periodical], 4 (Summer), 8-9.
History of field's development, simplified for outsiders.

1978

*C47   "Great Amber Questionnaire," <u>Hellride</u> [fanzine],
no. 3 (January 28), pp. 3-6. [Source: Zelazny.]
   Background on the Amber series, written for
group playing elaborate game based on the books.

 C48   Introductory comments scattered throughout <u>The
Illustrated Roger Zelazny</u>. [Publication date:
February.] <u>See</u> A113.

*C49   "A Conversation with Roger Zelazny" [interview
conducted by Terry Dowling and Keith Curtis],
<u>Science Fiction: A Review of Speculative Litera-
ture</u>, 1 (June), 11-23. [Source: Zelazny.]

*C50   "The Parts That Are Only Glimpsed: Three Re-
flexes," <u>SFWA Bulletin</u>, 13 (Summer), 14-16.

<u>Empire</u>, 4 (February 1979), 4-5.

 C51   "A Burnt-Out Case?," <u>SF Commentary</u> [fanzine],
no. 54 (November), pp. 22-28.
   Special Guest's Speech, Unicon, Easter 1978,
transcribed by Bruce Gillespie.

*C52   "Foreword" to <u>Other Worlds</u>, ed. Paul Collins.
Victoria, Australia: Void Publications, pp. 7-8.
[No publication date listed.] [Source: Zelazny.]

*C53   "Foreword" to <u>Rooms of Paradise</u>, ed. Lee Harding.
Melbourne, Australia: Quartet, pp. v-viii. [No
publication information available.] [Source:
Zelazny.]

Part C: Nonfiction

*C54   Brief appreciation of Philip José Farmer, <u>Norwescon 2 Program Booklet</u>, p. 7. [Convention was in March.] [Source: Zelazny.]

*C55   "Future Crime," <u>Future Life</u>, no. 10 (May), pp. 67–68. [Source: Zelazny.]

  C56   "Prologue" to <u>Empire of the East</u> by Fred Saberhagen. New York: Ace [publication date: October] [trade paperback], pp. vii–ix.

*C57   Review of <u>Sword of the Demon</u> (Lupoff), <u>Starlog's Science Fiction Yearbook</u>, 1 [published in October], p. 20. [Source: Zelazny.]

  C58   Brief response to a query in <u>Science Fiction and Fantasy Literature: A Checklist, 1700–1974 with Contemporary Science Fiction Authors II</u> by R. Reginald (pseud of Mike Burgess). Vol. 2. Detroit: Gale Research, p. 1137.

        Comment on the length of time involved in writing the Amber series.

Missing: Near the year 1969, Zelazny was co-editor (actually contributing editor, according to Zelazny) of <u>Nozdrovia</u>, fanzine edited by Richard Patt (source: Mark Owings). Zelazny contributed a short piece, title and subject of which now elude him.

Part D: Critical Studies

Part D lists major studies, substantial reviews, and brief but helpful references to Zelazny's work contained in larger critical works. Listing is alphabetical by author. Most of the items listed deal with Zelazny's books because of the obvious difficulty of tracking down every review of a magazine or anthology in which one of his stories appeared.

Basic listing is more inclusive than selective; I am aware enough of my personal bias to be reluctant to exclude a work because it appeared negligible to me. Therefore the list is as comprehensive as I could make it. The only items I have omitted intentionally are extremely brief capsule reviews, and I have been reluctant to do even that since sometimes--as do Buck Coulson's reviews in Yandro--they offer valid insights in a few sentences.

Annotation is as thorough as I considered necessary to give readers a fair summary of the writer's views. In a very few cases, I have offered my own estimation of those views in bracketed comments following the annotation. The lack of annotation of a work that has been seen is also a comment on its value. Whenever possible, I have used quotations to let writers speak for themselves, showing effectively worded perceptions or, sometimes, le mot injuste. Page numbers are cited for quotes from essays of ten pages or longer.

Part D: Critical Studies

At the risk of inconsistency I have annotated earlier reviews more heavily, to show Zelazny's initial critical reception.

Information on most unseen items is from Hall Hall's Science Fiction Book Review Index (primary volume and annual supplements).

1966

D1   Ashley, Mike. "Roger Zelazny." Cosign [fanzine] no. 5 (November-December), pp. 5-7.
        Labels Zelazny as greatest talent of decade. Summarizes Zelazny's writing career, listing publications and quoting reader comments in Amazing and Fantastic letter columns.

*D2   Bailey, H. Review of This Immortal. New Worlds, no. 169 (December), p. 153. [Source: Hall.]

D3   Bangsund, John. Review of This Immortal. Australian Science Fiction Review [fanzine], no. 4 (October), pp. 25-26.
        Calls Conrad "a superb creation," likes Zelazny's humor; only disappointment is that book is too short.

D4   Budrys, Algis. Review of This Immortal. Galaxy, 25 (December), 131-133.
        Discusses book as part of new interest in classical sources. Conrad represents Greek ideal--understands duty even in midst of struggle with disaster. Hassan used "to provide a contrast between the educated deadly man and the killing machine." Major problem solved too easily. Approves large, optimistic vision; book is "based on thoroughly understood, inexhaustible engagements with one's own grasp" (cf. Robert Browning's philosophy).

D5   Coulson, Robert. Review of The Dream Master.
Yandro [fanzine], no. 163 (n.d.), pp. 10-11.
    Mentions other stories with similar theme--
Brunner's The Whole Man and Peter Phillips's
"Dreams are Sacred."

D6   Gilliland, Alexis. Review of The Dream Master.
The WSFA Journal [fanzine], no. 32 (mid-October),
p. 3.
    Calls this work a rhapsody in prose, with lit-
tle plot but "155 pages of splendid characters
and fascinating detail." Contrasts to This Immortal. Praises story's virtuosity, but considers
it to be less than Zelazny is capable of.

D7   Gilliland, Alexis A. Review of This Immortal.
The WSFA Journal [fanzine], no. 25 (July), p. 3.

D8   Merrill, Judith. Review of This Immortal. F&SF,
31 (December), 33-35.
    Impressive for poetry, technical skill, "oc-
casional philosophic insights and character
asides," but "disappointing as a novel, both in
conception and structure." Reactionary in attempting to reintroduce myths rather than accept
their demise. Beyond conventional plot and confusing thematic inversions, style is unusual:
"alternatively intensely-intimately-tender and
tough-hard-boiled in mood, essentially introspec-
tive in tone, much more preoccupied with personal
moralities and ethics than group mores or behavior." Compares to Hammett-Chandler school of
detective fiction.

D9   White, Ted. "With Jaundiced Eye" [column].
Yandro [fanzine], no. 162 (August), pp. 6-11.
    Section entitled "Significance & Science Fic-
tion" discusses Zelazny at Disclave '58. Largely
White's argument against conscious straining after
importance; favors instinctive storytelling.

Quotes Zelazny: "I never know how a story will come out. 'Conrad' was supposed to be a tragedy; I didn't expect him to save the whole damned world. When I hit a difficult spot, I'll get up, put on a record of the sort of music that hits the mood I want to create, and maybe pace for an hour. Sometimes I just go to bed. I've dreamed about my characters. They're as real to me as you are."

1967

D10   Ballard, J. G. "The Year's Science Fiction" [review of Nebula Award Stories 2 (ed. Brian Aldiss and Harry Harrison), This Immortal, Babel-17 (Samuel Delany), and An Age (Brian Aldiss)]. The Guardian, 29 December. [Source: British newspaper reviews in Zelazny's clipping file, now in possession of Syracuse U and UMBC.]

Virtually same review appears in Manchester Guardian Weekly, 4 January 1968, p. 11, under title "Generations of SF." [Source: Zelazny's clipping files.]
Calls Zelazny and Delany "talented recruits to the old school" of sf writing.

D11   Budrys, Algis. Review of Four for Tomorrow. Galaxy, 25 (August), 139–140.
Zelazny is at beginning of what would be peak of achievement for most writers. Compares this book to Three Stories by Murray Leinster, Jack Williamson, and John Wyndham (ed. Sam Moskowitz).

D12   Budrys, Algis. "Galaxy Bookshelf" [review column]. Galaxy, 26 (October), 188–194.
Contains several references to Zelazny during discussion of new group of writers. (Einstein Intersection [Delany] is primary book under review.)

*D13 Cawthorn, J. Review of <u>The Dream Master</u>. <u>New Worlds</u>, no. 170 (January), p. 155. [Source: Hall.]

*D14 Cawthorn, J. Review of <u>Four for Tomorrow</u>. <u>New Worlds</u>, no. 173 (July), p. 63. [Source: Hall.]

D15 Cooper, Edmund. "Science Fiction" [review of <u>This Immortal</u>, <u>Babel-17</u> (Samuel Delany), <u>Nebula Award Stories 2</u> (ed. Brian Aldiss and Harry Harrison), and <u>New Writings in SF</u> (ed. Edward J. Carnell)]. Sunday <u>Times</u> (London), 10 December. [Source: Zelazny's clippings file.]
  Zelazny may be short on science, but he manipulates myth compellingly.

D16 Coulson, Robert. Review of <u>Four for Tomorrow</u>. <u>Yandro</u> [fanzine], no. 168 (February), p. 24.

D17 Delap, Richard. Review of <u>Lord of Light</u>. <u>Yandro</u> [fanzine], no. 177 (December), pp. 6-7.
  Can't decide whether Zelazny meant to write merely fantastic adventure or attempt more serious allegory; in any event, finds the novel "an inane mishmash." Highly upset by "nauseously aggravating" word games and incongruities in style.

D18 Ellison, Harlan. "Introduction" to "Auto-da-fe." In <u>Dangerous Visions</u>, ed. Harlan Ellison. Garden City, N.Y.: Doubleday [publication date: 20 October, pp. 499-500.
  Enthusiastic praise, explaining Zelazny's youthful accomplishments by his being "the reincarnation of Geoffrey Chaucer."

D19 Gilliland, Alexis A. Review of <u>Four for Tomorrow</u>. <u>The WSFA Journal</u> [fanzine], no. 42 (May), p. 17.
  Zelazny is developing more complex, less intelligible writing. Style is becoming private, a barrier to communication.

D20   Harding, Lee. Review of Starshine (Theodore
      Sturgeon) and Four for Tomorrow. Australian
      Science Fiction Review [fanzine], no. 10 (n.d.),
      pp. 61-63.
          Actually uses Zelazny as foil for discussion
      of Sturgeon's struggles as a writer: terrific
      immediate impact, several (flawed) gems of sto-
      ries, currently challenged to stay on course.

D21   Hillman, Martin. "SF" [capsule reviews of Babel-
      17 (Samuel Delany), This Immortal, Three Novels
      (Damon Knight), The Door into Summer (Robert A.
      Heinlein), Nebula Award Stories 2 (ed. Brian
      Aldiss and Harry Harrison), and brief mentions of
      other books]. The Tribune (London?), 22 December.
      [Source: Zelazny's clipping file.]
          Conrad an archetypal hero. Zelazny a major
      innovator of sf; his "assured knowledge of myth,
      and his expert, oblique insertions of it into his
      story, elevate the novel far above any run-of-the
      mill adventure yarn in SF costume."

D22   Klein, Jay Kay. "Lunacon/Eastercon 1967." The
      WSFA Journal [fanzine], no. 43 (June), pp. 3-10.
          Discusses Zelazny's appearance at sf conven-
      tion, with anecdotes about career, comment on
      writing procedures.

D23   [Laber, J. M. C.]. Review of This Immortal. Bucks
      Standard (Newport Pagnell), 15 December.

      Also in Wilts & Gloucestershire Standard,
          29 December. [Source: Zelazny's clipping
          file.

D24   McGuinness, Frank. "Books" [review of This Im-
      mortal]. Queen, 13 December. [Source: Zelazny's
      clipping file.]

D25 Miller, P. Schuyler. Review of <u>Four for Tomorrow</u>.
<u>Analog</u>, 80 (October), 165–166.
  "With Cordwainer Smith's death . . . , Zelazny
certainly stands alone as the most unusual and
promising of the newer American SF writers."
Calls the book a "must."

D26 Nightengale, Benedict. "Science Fiction" [review
of <u>The Best Science Fiction Stories of Clifford
Simak, This Immortal, Nebula Award Stories 2</u> (ed.
Brian Aldiss and Harry Harrison), <u>Babel-17</u>
(Samuel Delany), <u>The Door into Summer</u> (Robert A.
Heinlein), and <u>Three Novels</u> (Damon Knight)]. <u>The
Observer</u> (London), 17 December. [Source:
Zelazny's clipping file.]

D27 Norton, Andre. "Roger Zelazny." <u>The WSFA Journal</u> [fanzine], no. 47 (October), p. 7.
  Brief expression of awe. Printed with bibliography slightly longer than a page. Editor
notes that both are reprinted from Macon II Program Book, bibliography "condensed and updated."

D28 O'Connell, John. "The New Novels" [review of <u>The
Fair Ladies of Salamanca</u> (David Walder), <u>Hawkwood</u>
(Hubert Cole), <u>The Spinsters</u> (John Williams),
<u>Michael, Michael</u> (Robert Lewis), <u>A Case of Nullity</u>
(Evelyn Berckman), and <u>This Immortal</u>]. <u>The Irish
Press</u> (Dublin), 23 December. [Source: Zelazny's
clipping file.]

*D29 Panshin, Alexei. Review of <u>This Immortal</u>.
<u>Nyarlathotep</u> [fanzine], no. 4. [Source: Referred to by Zelazny in "De Gustibus," <u>see</u> C7.]

D30 Skinner, Olivia. "Fantastic Convention." <u>St.
Louis Post-Dispatch</u>, 8 August, p. 30.
  Write-up on Ozarkon, with description of
Zelazny's speech, some quotes from a brief interview. Photo of Zelazny.

D31   Sturgeon, Theodore. "Introduction" to <u>Four for</u>
       <u>Tomorrow</u>. New York: Ace, pp. 7-12.
           Stresses Zelazny's uniqueness in and outside
       sf: a genuine prose poet--who's also a "truly
       great story teller"--who also can "create memor-
       able characters"--who also can master "structure
       and content." Beyond that, praises Zelazny's
       work because it is literally fabulous; like
       fables, stories go beyond particular circum-
       stances to strike larger truths. Also, though
       critical of stylistic tricks and esoteric refer-
       ences that bring a reader up short and thus
       interfere with communication, praises Zelazny's
       willingness to experiment by taking chances;
       concludes that Zelazny "is young and already a
       giant; he has the habit of hard work and of
       learning, and shows no slightest sign of slowing
       down or of being diverted." Sturgeon ranks these
       stories in order of increasing merit: "The Doors
       of His Face, The Lamps of His Mouth," "The
       Furies," "The Graveyard Heart," and above all "A
       Rose for Ecclesiastes."
           [Personal reaction rather than critical analy-
       sis, but very perceptive on that level.]

                            1968

D32   Anon. "Do You Mind?" [review of <u>The Dream Mas-</u>
       <u>ter</u>, <u>Starshine</u> (Sturgeon), <u>New Writings in S-F 11</u>
       (ed. Edward J. Carnell), <u>The Werewolf Principle</u>
       (Clifford Simak), <u>Undersea Fleet</u> (Frederik Pohl
       and Jack Williamson), <u>Star Man's Son</u> (Andre
       Norton), and <u>The Wind Obeys Lama Toru</u> (Lee Tung)].
       <u>Times Literary Supplement</u>, 8 March, p. 310.
           Criticizes obtrusive style but still calls "an
       intelligent and basically simple story," diluted
       by "fragments of older legends." Characters like
       Render's son or Eileen's dog limited, can't grow.

D33   Anon. Review of <u>Lord of Light</u>. <u>Times Literary
       Supplement</u>, 29 February. [Source: Zelazny's
       clipping file.]
           "A weird allegorical fantasy which sets out to
       demonstrate how self-destructive is the human
       compulsion to create gods and demons." Calls it
       "far-fetched." Disapproves of mixed style. Won-
       ders whether it's intended as a parody.

D34   Ballard, J. G. "Generations of SF." <u>See</u> D10.

D35   Christopher, John. "Not What-If But How-He."
       <u>The Writer</u>, 81 (November), 15-17, 45.
           Refers to Zelazny as natural successor to
       Cordwainer Smith in creating "Far Out" sf, "ut-
       terly strange and . . . set a long time in the
       future." Cites "He Who Shapes" as example.

*D36   Colvin, J. Review of <u>Lord of Light</u>. <u>New Worlds</u>,
       no. 178 (December-January), p. 61. [Source:
       Hall.]

D37   Cooper, Edmund. Review of <u>Lord of Light</u>. <u>The
       Sunday Times</u> (London), 18 February. [Source:
       Zelazny's clipping file.]
           "The narrative is at times hazy. At times it
       is also brilliant and written with impact. . . .
       Entertaining and original concepts."

D38   Haden-Guest, Anthony. "S.F. Goes All Baroque"
       [review of <u>Babel-17</u> (Samuel Delany), <u>This Immor-
       tal</u>, <u>An Age</u> (Brian Aldiss), <u>A Van Vogt Omnibus</u>,
       <u>Three Novels</u> (Damon Knight), <u>Best Science Fiction
       Stories of Clifford Simak</u>, and <u>Mister Da V</u> (Kit
       Reed)]. <u>Sunday's Telegraph</u> (London), 7 January.
       [Source: Zelazny's clipping file.]
           Despite exotic looks, Conrad "comes on a bit
       like Deighton's Harry Palmer."

D39   [Laker, J. H. C.]. Review of <u>Lord of Light</u>. <u>Bucks</u>
      <u>Standard</u> (Newport Pagnell), 15 March. [Source:
      Zelazny's clipping file.]

D40   Masters, Norman E. "After the Fanfare Dies"
      [editorial]. <u>No-Eyed Monster</u> [fanzine], no. 13
      (n.d.), pp. 4-7.
         Summary of Zelazny's talk at Triple-Fan Fair.

D41   Mebane, Banks. "Gunpowder I' the Court, Wildfire
      at Midnight." <u>Algol</u> [fanzine], no. 13 (June),
      pp. 39-45.
         Analysis of Zelazny's prose, discovering that
      the "yoking together of very different ideas is
      like the techniques of the so-called 'metaphysi-
      cal' poets of the seventeenth century--Donne,
      Herbert, Vaughan, Marvell, and company--and the
      baroque dramatists like Chapman, Tournier, and
      Webster." Discusses specific metaphors from
      Zelazny's work as metaphysical comparisons,
      bringing apparently disparate ideas together, as
      revitalization of cliché, showing that apparently
      figurative statements are literally true, and as
      tightly packed visual passages, speeding up the
      description. Also comments on puns, as appro-
      priate to the story or not, as well as literary
      references. Concludes that "fiction writers who
      are so concerned with compression of thought and
      verbal decoration usually turn out clotted,
      static stories. Zelazny's talent amazes one the
      more, for beneath these surface ripples the cur-
      rents and creatures of the deeps still move and
      hold."
         [A key early critical essay; note also letters
      to the editor in <u>Algol</u> no. 14 (Fall), for com-
      ments on Mebane's essay.]

D42   Miesel, Sandra. "Love is Madness." <u>Kallikanzaros</u>
        [fanzine], no. 4 (March-April), pp. 6-11.
           Analysis of myth-symbolism in <u>The Dream Master</u>.
        Identifies several sources but points out that
        Zelazny does not stick to one: "No motif, not
        even the dominant one of Tristan and Isolde, is
        treated consistently or in full. Opposite images
        shimmer, melt, and blend into one another without
        discordance." In addition to quick references on
        Zelazny's part, myth is discussed overtly in the
        novel, as Render consciously considers enthusiasm
        for it "a retreat from modern reality in search
        of meaning and value." Nonetheless, novel uses
        myth to deepen impact of action, to make universal
        its relevance. Bulk of essay is detailed explica-
        tion of myths used in the novel, leading to con-
        clusion that "the man who scoffed at Dostoevsky's
        hell 'is the suffering of being unable love . . .'
        falls into the Abyss which his own lovelessness
        has created. . . . Render refuses love as madness;
        therefore in madness he perishes."
           [Admirably detailed analysis. Note Zelazny's
        letter, <u>see</u> C17, which accepts Miesel's identifi-
        cation and analysis.]

D43   Miller, P. Schuyler. Review of <u>Lord of Light</u>.
        <u>Analog</u>, 81 (June), 160-161.
           Possible to confuse story with straight sfish
        retelling of Hindu myths, so spends most of time
        explaining background. Calls this work "a unique
        blend of myth and mirth, legend and jarring anach-
        ronism." Again praises Zelazny for not repeating
        self.

D44   Nightengale, Benedict. Review of <u>The Dream Mas-
        ter</u>. <u>The Observer Review</u>, 14 April. [Source:
        Zelazny's clipping file.]
           Zelazny has no better than a layman's knowledge
        of psychology, but "does seem to know something

about the arrogance of power. . . . So much for
over-reaching ambition--an old, dour puritan
lesson in contemporary wrapping."

D45   Nightengale, Benedict.   Review of Lord of Light.
The Observer (London), 25 February. [Source:
Zelazny's clipping file.]
      "A skittish foray into speculative theology.
. . . Zelazny takes this mischievous notion
imaginatively, if rather self-indulgently,
luxuriating in archaic language."

D46   Redfern, Paul. "The Future: From the Past and
the Present" [review of Best S.F. Stories of
C. M. Kornbluth, The Iron Thorn (Algis Budrys),
Lord of Light, and The Dome (Gonner Jones)]. New
Scientist, 37 (21 March), 652.
      Describes Lord of Light as "a long and tortuous
work with shades of C. S. Lewis in its mixture of
religious fantasy and magical acts with heavy al-
legories," also "an original and highly imagina-
tive book, but it is demanding of time and
patience." Criticizes for length, loose writing,
and sophomoric philosophy.

D47   Reed, David. "'Les Mots': Never Question
Roses." L'Angue Jacque [fanzine], no. 2
(October), pp. 17-18.
      Billed as first of three-part study of
"Zelazny's most acclaimed works, including his
novels The Dream Master, This Immortal, and Lord
of Light." This section deals with "A Rose for
Ecclesiastes." Gallinger considers self above
other humans, but Martians "by fulfilling his
subconscious need to be impressed . . . allow
him to drop his conceit as a now useless protec-
tion." Compares dance to Eliot's description in
"Burnt Norton."

D48   [Rottensteiner, Franz?]. Review of <u>Lord of</u>
      <u>Light</u>. <u>Quarber Merkur</u>, 6 (April), 56–57.

D49   Russ, Joanna. Review of <u>Lord of Light</u>. <u>F&SF</u>, 34
      (January), 37–38.
            Calls this work seven episodes, not a whole
      novel. Brilliant evocation of mythic images and
      rational explanation. But only in background
      lurk "the personal stories of . . . [the] in-
      habitants of Heaven, the actual colonization, the
      effect upon human beings of immortality and the
      Aspects and Attributes of the superhuman, a real
      conflict of philosophies and attitudes." As this
      becomes more interesting, foreground action seems
      irrelevant; characters less than they appear.
      "Will Zelazny ever write the inside stories of
      his stories? Can he?"

D50   Stableford, Brian. Review of <u>Lord of Light</u>.
      <u>Speculation</u> [fanzine], no. 17 (February),
      pp. 24–26.
            Finds this more ambitious than Zelazny's
      earlier works, sometimes too complex; as example,
      cites Sam's discovery that the "true" Buddha ob-
      scures picture of religion rather than offering
      Zelazny's view of religious "values and reali-
      ties." "Zelazny appears to cast Christianity in
      a particularly harsh role, but this would appear
      to be a matter of expediency, since he never
      questions the 'truths' of religions and merely
      judges their systematics." Novel falters because
      too ambitious and gimmicky.

D51   Tanner, L. [Harry Harrison?]. Review of <u>Lord of</u>
      <u>Light</u>. <u>Amazing</u>, 41 (February), 141–142.
            Hates style: Zelazny "has an unenviable tal-
      ent for <u>inventing</u> cliches."

D52   Young, B. A. "Space Time" [reviews of Lord of
       Light and The Dream Master]. Punch, 3 April.
       [Source: Zelazny's clipping file.]
          Lord of Light is "all atmosphere and no sub-
       stance." In The Dream Master, "the tense atmo-
       sphere is artificially created by the sequences
       of three and four-word paragraphs and if normally
       deployed would evaporate."

                          1969

D53   Bangsund, John. Review of Isle of the Dead. SF
       Commentary [fanzine], no. 5 (August), pp. 38-40.
          Finds book enjoyable on action level. How-
       ever, finds Sandow "too far removed from the
       grubby realities of everyday life" to be an ac-
       ceptable hero. "Sandow's closest counterpart is
       the rich, dilettante amateur detective . . . who
       has no cause at all to go about righting wrongs--
       except for our entertainment." More than two
       dimensional but not fully integrated character.

D54   Budrys, Algis. Review of Creatures of Light and
       Darkness. Galaxy, 29 (November), 141-142.
          Concepts and events in book aren't related to
       our own time; we must apply our minds to a story
       "full of adventure and poetry, lacking guideposts
       but possessing a nearly perfect clarity." Ad-
       mires achievement, but thinks one work like this
       is enough.

D55   Budrys, Algis. Review of Isle of the Dead.
       Galaxy, 28 (March), 187-190.
          Discusses economic and time pressures that af-
       fect writing of paperback originals, before con-
       cluding that Zelazny was inspired, did fine job.

D56   Budrys, Algis. <u>Review of Nebula Award Stories</u>
<u>Three</u>. <u>Galaxy</u>, 28 (May), 137–139.
    Takes Zelazny to task for "block of marbelized
verbiage" with "canned-brains clichés" in his introduction and afterword.

*D57   Churchill, J. Review of <u>Nebula Award Stories</u>
<u>Three</u>. <u>New Worlds</u>, no. 186 (January), p. 62.
[Source: Hall.]

*D58   Delany, Samuel R. "Faust and Archimedes." <u>SFWA</u>
<u>Forum</u> [fanzine], August, pp. 15–26.
    Essay on Thomas M. Disch and Zelazny. De-
scribes basic standard of judgment in sf as ingenu-
ity of idea, giving reader something to think about.
"The minimum standard had nothing to do with liter-
acy, and only barely defined the intelligible"
(p. 16). Comments that one problem in sf critics'
reaction to Zelazny and Disch is that much recent sf
has paralleled mainstream literature in naturalistic
narrative techniques. But more recently, with advent
of sf-influence mainstream writers such as Lawrence
Durrell, John Barth, and Donald Barthelme, more emphasis on flexible style to fit content. Delany relates Disch and Zelazny to contemporary literature,
especially to symbolism, which he classifies as:
(1) reductive symbolism that strips narrative to
its bones, the better to reveal hidden structural
relationships; and (2) intensive symbolism that
heightens immediate perception of life by vivid,
concentrated language. "Zelazny's pastiche of
Cordwainer Smith, 'The Furies,' and his forth-
coming novel <u>Creatures of Light and Darkness</u> are
essentially reductive. 'He Who Shapes' and the
first-person novels and novellas are the most
elegant examples of intensive symbolism in American prose" (p. 19). Discusses Zelazny's treat-
ment of immortality: rather than leading to
satiety, opens appreciation of each moment--a
justification for the intensively symbolic language. Appreciates Zelazny's ability to communi-

cate hunger for life. (Qualifies Mebane [see D41] by emphasizing that Zelazny manages to create metaphysical images in "rhythms of contemporary American" (p. 21). Specifically discusses striving and failure of central characters in "A Rose for Ecclesiastes" and "He Who Shapes" (also comments on differences between original version of latter story and its revision into the book-length The Dream Master).

Delany asserts sf is "the only area of literature outside poetry that is symbolistic in its basic conception. Its stated aim is to represent the world without reproducing it" (p. 19). What sf represents is "the human responsibility that comes from the acquisition of knowledge" (p. 20), as in the case of Faust. Unites Faustian theme with discussion of symbolism by considering stories as models for human consciousness. Zelazny responds to human condition and knowledge by symbolically insisting that "We must become receptors to every nuance and shading of both the inner and the outer, to make ourselves worthy of the immortality we all seek (in one level or another). . . . A corollary to this answer is a warning that if we allow ourselves any less, than richness, death--either spiritual or real--is the alternative" (p. 24). Contrasting to Disch's more complex mode, Delany points out that Zelazny recognizes that "organizational" obstacles to personal salvation actually are the projected reality of . . . wounded individualists" (p. 24). Praises both authors as makers of meaningful models.

[Remarkable essay, going beyond specific analysis/reactions and sf-field criticism; a vital starting point in Zelazny criticism. Fortunately, available in slightly revised form in The Jewel-Hinged Jaw: Notes on the Language of Science Fiction. Elizabethtown, New York: Dragon Press, 1977; New York: Berkley, 1978 (paper).]

D59 Gillespie, Bruce. Review of <u>Nebula Award Stories
Three</u>. <u>SF Commentary</u> [fanzine], no. 4 (July),
pp. 41-48.
Primarily a discussion of what's considered
"good" sf these days. Remarks that Zelazny's
commentary doesn't explain basis of choice.

D60 Gilliland, Alexis. Review of <u>Isle of the Dead</u>.
<u>The WSFA Journal</u> [fanzine], no. 66 (April-May),
p. 57.
Calls this Zelazny's best work yet. Simple
plot but interesting decorations. Sandow is
Zelazny's richest, most complex character, with
fascinating sidemen. Style less private, less
Baroque than in past; symbolism doesn't get in
way of story.

D61 Holmberg, John-Henri. "Et Karleksbrev." <u>Mentat</u>
[fanzine], no. 11 (May), pp. 204-208.
Essay in German, with partial bibliography.

D62 Hubbard, Gary N. "Don't Touch that Dial! It's
Time for the Late, Late Roger Zelazny." <u>Trumpet</u>
[fanzine], no. 10 (n.d.), p. 48. [Reprinted from
<u>Beabohema</u>, no. 1; no other information given.]
Feels that Zelazny could have made it as a
movie writer in Hollywood of the 1930s. "In
truth the only difference between Zelazny's writ-
ing and that found in the pulps is simply: [sic]
Zelazny's is purpler. . . . Roger Zelazny writes
old movies with science fictional trimmings."
Comments on "The Doors of His Face, The Lamps of
His Mouth," "And Call Me Conrad," "The Graveyard
Heart," "The Furies," and "Damnation Alley."

D63 Merrill, Judith. Discussion of <u>Isle of the Dead</u>
(along with <u>Stand on Zanzibar</u> [John Brunner], <u>The
Two Timers</u> [Bob Shaw], and <u>Goblin Reservation</u>
[Clifford Simak]. <u>F&SF</u>, 36 (February), 22-25.

    Focuses on Zelazny's achieving deep resonances
from "comic-book images." Believes Zelazny is
getting away from fascination with clever sur-
faces.

D64   Miller, P. Schuyler. Review of <u>Isle of the Dead</u>.
<u>Analog</u>, 84 (December), 166-167.
    Points out influence of John W. Campbell, Jr.
(editor of <u>Analog</u>) on sf, so that psi stories can
be considered legitimate--even when narrator
calls self a "god."

D65   Miller, P. Schuyler. Review of <u>Nebula Award
Stories Three</u>. <u>Analog</u>, 83 (July), 164.

D66   Schaumburger, Joe. Review of <u>Lord of Light</u>.
<u>Luna Monthly</u> [fanzine], no. 7 (December), p. 29.
    "A little mystical and hard to follow in
spots, but well worth the effort."

D67   Slavin, Jan. Review of <u>Isle of the Dead</u>. <u>Luna
Monthly</u> [fanzine], no. 2 (July), p. 27.
    "Marvelous and maddening." Rouses sense of
wonder, but unsure of meaning.

D68   White, Ted. Review of <u>Isle of the Dead</u>.
<u>Fantastic</u>, 18 (August), 130-132.
    Zelazny "has been working his way almost
methodically through the folklore of many nation-
alities in his books. . . . [In <u>Isle of the
Dead</u>] he creates a wholly new, alien, mythology . . . and builds and resolves his conflict
through this living mythology." A great personal
achievement that this is as convincing as other
works. Finds book transmuted version of John D.
MacDonald's Travis McGee novels. Discusses
Sandow's belief/disbelief in god outside himself. Calls book moving--more than thriller.

1970

D69   Anon. Review of Creatures of Light and Darkness.
      The Bookseller, 8 August.

D70   Anon. Review of Creatures of Light and Darkness.
      Evening News (Manchester), 10 December. [Source:
      Zelazny's clipping file.]
          "No current writer can add to the myth or add
      to his own stature by putting modern English idiom
      into the mouths of immense, cloudy figures from
      the ancient Egyptian pantheon."

D71   Anon. Review of Creatures of Light and Darkness.
      Evening News (London), 12 December. [Source:
      Zelazny's clipping file.]

D72   Anon. Review of Creatures of Light and Darkness.
      Keighley News (Keighley, Yorkshire), 11 December.
      [Source: Zelazny's clipping file.]
          Stresses violence, calls this work "bizarre
      coagulation."

D73   Anon. Review of Damnation Alley. Publishers
      Weekly, 197 (11 May), 44.

D74   Anon. Review of Nine Princes in Amber. Pub-
      lishers Weekly, 197 (27 April), 79.
          "There isn't one character or one place in this
      confusing novel to whom one can relate. . . . A
      little-league version of Conan."

D75   Anon. Review of Nine Princes in Amber. The
      Booklist, 67 (15 September), 84.

D76   Blish, James. Review of Creatures of Light and
      Darkness. F&SF, 38 (April), 49-51.
          Relates novel to: (1) T. S. Eliot's sugges-
      tion that myth might take place of structure or
      plot; and (2) New Wave experimentation.

Nonetheless, labels it "a flat failure." Faults conception for "its primary assumption that the Egyptian gods were real creatures with real powers to control the universe" and for out-of-character behavior by these gods. Also attacks inconsistent tone of style. Moreover, criticizes form for scrappiness, confusion, and lack of clear narrative line. Finally, faults Zelazny for confusing myth's appeal to changeless forces with sf's emphasis on change; by evoking names of gods, "you are writing an allegory whether you want to or not, and if you don't even realize that this is the problem, the end product is bound to ring false."

D77   Brodsky, Allyn B. Review of Creatures of Light and Darkness. Luna Monthly [fanzine], no. 16 (September), p. 25.
         Compares this work to Lord of Light. Creatures lacks central character for empathy; characters distant from readers, sometimes possessing "monumental power of Egyptian art," though this impression is jarred by slang. Some scenes in overall mosaic are majestic, some read like put-ons. Part of the style "almost an epic from an oral tradition," part like self-parody.

D78   Clark, Collin. Review of Damnation Alley. Library Journal, 95 (15 January), 260.

D79   Davis, Jo-Ann. Review of Anywhere (James Blish) and Nine Princes in Amber. Library Journal, 95 (July), 2513.
         "Not only a suspenseful, intriguing fantasy, but also an allegory concerning man's alienation and consequent search for meaning and identity." Corwin alienated not by evil but by "feelings of kinship and humanity, which have ceased to exist among mankind."

D80   Delap, Richard. Review of <u>Damnation Alley</u>.
        <u>Science Fiction Review</u> [fanzine], no. 39 (August),
        pp. 31–32.
            Summary, designed to expose book's violence,
        stylistic pretentiousness.

D81   del Rey, Lester. Review of <u>Nine Princes in Amber</u>.
        <u>If</u>, 20 (November–December), 165–167.
            Calls attention to Zelazny's borrowing from
        myth but also labels his work "high creation."
        Largely an attack on publishers who foist incom-
        plete novels on public.

D82   Gilliland, Alexis. Review of <u>Damnation Alley</u>.
        <u>The WSFA Journal</u> [fanzine], no. 72 (June–August),
        pp. 20–21.
            Admires writing but dislikes book, citing
        trite plot, unconvincing hero (standard Zelazny
        hero in costume), flawed background and technical
        details.

D83   Hartridge, Jon. "SF" [review of <u>In Our Hands the
        Stars</u> (Harry Harrison) and <u>Creatures of Light and
        Darkness</u>]. <u>Oxford Mail</u> (Oxford, Oxfordshire),
        17 December. [Source: Zelazny's clipping file.]
            Stresses violence and "regurgitated mishmash
        of half absorbed legends," but finds "extremely
        readable."

D84   Keller, Donald G. Review of <u>Creatures of Light
        and Darkness</u>. <u>Phantasmicom</u> [fanzine], no. 3
        (Summer), pp. 33–34.
            Calls this Zelazny's best novel.

D85   Keller, Donald G. Review of <u>Damnation Alley</u>.
        <u>Phantasmicom</u> [fanzine], no. 3 (Summer), 34–35.
            Readable but beneath Zelazny's ability; com-
        pares to Norman Spinrad.

D86   Keller, Donald G. Review of <u>Nine Princes in</u>
       <u>Amber</u>. <u>Beabohema</u> [fanzine], no. 16 (June),
       pp. 20-21.
           Delighted by first half, finds rest too
       rushed--Amber too little realized. Speculates
       lapse may be because book was half-written more
       than three years earlier, taken up later.

D87   Malzberg, Barry. Review of <u>Damnation Alley</u>.
       <u>F&SF</u>, 38 (May), 26-27.
           "The flaw of the novella was that it had no
       characterological interior or sense of pace; and
       instead of concentrating this novelization on
       those areas which might have done some good (like
       ironic counterpoint) Zelazny has simply souped up
       and extended the action." Sees some hope in fact
       that Zelazny doesn't repeat self, keeps trying
       new things.
           [Whatever validity of comments, based on se-
       riously inaccurate plot summary.]

D88   Meadley, R. G. Review of <u>Isle of the Dead</u>.
       <u>Speculation</u> [fanzine], no. 27 (September-October),
       p. 20.
           Calls novel underdeveloped heap of ideas:
       "Had less space been wasted on babbling inanity,
       less effort on trying to cram in Donne, Weber,
       Jung and God knows who else (a <u>melange</u> of ir-
       relevant high-school cultural reference), and
       more time spent developing the anyway mediocre
       plot, this might have made a reasonable romp."

D89   Panshin, Alexei. "Books in the Field: Science
       Fiction." <u>Wilson Library Bulletin</u>, 44 (February),
       616-620.
           Cites Zelazny and Delany as paradigms for
       current sf.

D90   Parkinson, Bob. Review of <u>A Rose for Ecclesias-</u>
       <u>tes</u> [British edition of <u>Four for Tomorrow</u>] and
       <u>Isle of the Dead</u>. <u>Speculation</u> [fanzine], no. 26
       (May), pp. 32-34.
           Many of characters are superhuman, but
       Zelazny's "heroes are not believers. . . . They
       are twentieth-century agnostics caught up in the
       myth that lies beneath the surface of his
       stories."
           [Within limits of brief review, a very sharp
       perception of content of these works and of
       Zelazny's general themes.]

D91   Pauls, Ted. Review of <u>Isle of the Dead</u>. <u>River-</u>
       <u>side Quarterly</u> [fanzine], no. 4 (June), pp. 208-
       209.
           Basically a lucid plot summary, with comments
       on hero's wry outlook as result of long life
       experience.

D92   Pauls, T. Review of <u>Nebula Award Stories Three</u>.
       <u>WSFA Journal</u> [fanzine], 74 (December 1970-
       January 1971), 36-37.

D93   Pierce, John J. Review of <u>Damnation Alley</u>. <u>Luna</u>
       <u>Monthly</u> [fanzine], no. 16 (September), pp. 26-27.
           Calls Zelazny a "master of expressionist
       mythology," <u>Damnation Alley</u> a "parable of moral
       salvations." Chaos of wrecked America symbolic
       of chaos inside Tanner as result of his rejecting
       humanity and moral standards. Journey is strug-
       gle to get out of spiritual shell; duty vs.
       natural chaos. An epic.

D94   J. J. P. [John J. Pierce]. Review of <u>Creatures</u>
       <u>of Light and Darkness</u> and <u>Damnation Alley</u>. <u>Re-</u>
       <u>naissance</u> [fanzine], 2 (Winter), 11.
           Speaks of Zelazny as savior of "Romanticism"
       (optimistic, human-centered viewpoint) in sf of
       1960s. Labels <u>Creatures</u> self-parody, uneasy in

tone because Zelazny realizes he has more important things to say. Finds message in Damnation
Alley to be "salavation through acceptance of
moral duty," as Tanner overcomes dark forces in
his soul and "wins the reader's forgiveness--and
even admiration--at the end of his epic journey."

D95   Rottensteiner, Franz. Review of A Rose for Ecclesiastes [British ed. of Four for Tomorrow] and
Isle of the Dead. Speculation [fanzine], no. 26
(May), pp. 29-31.
        Calls writing skillful but empty: "The 'Tokyo
Bay philosophy' and some sentimentalizing about
love and death is about the utmost you'll get; or
perhaps some old myth, banalized and warmed-up
for easy digestion; never to be compared with the
original creation." Myth is acceptable in The
Dream Master, within characters' minds, but we
can't believe in physical existence of gods.
Zelazny also enmeshed in "ritual of American pulp
literature"--individualism and similar delusions.
Condemns froth and clichés. Calls Gallinger ego
projection of Zelazny--doesn't have to be best
poet in the world to do what he does. Links
Zelazny to Alfred Bester as deceptively impressive; contrasts unfavorably to Disch, who better
fits our times. Calls Zelazny's popularity a
sign of fans' immaturity.

D96   Schweitzer, Darrell. Review of Nine Princes in
Amber. Renaissance [fanzine], 2 (Summer), 16.
        Finds novel interesting but unsuccessful be-
cause of superficial characterization, "hurried
plot." Overall book fails to show what makes
Amber special, Eric evil.

D97   Walker, Paul. Review of Creatures of Light and
Darkness. Science Fiction Review [fanzine],
no. 35 (February), pp. 28-29.
        Compares Zelazny to John Updike: each "creates
a work that is impressive, that intimates with its

intellect and aesthetics, and [yet] . . . there
is that curious hollowness about his work." Delight in act of writing, without much content
(appropriate for our time, which is not conducive
to great themes). Book stresses put-down of re-
ligion as "humorously cynical. . . . Man is the
best god there ever was. He is more decent, more
rational, more humane than any god there ever
was. And his universe is more intriguing, more
incredible, more spectacular than any heaven
there ever was. To live is the point." However,
novel is unpretentious finally because it's not
really about anything except Zelazny's ability to
use words interestingly.
[Perceptive on the novel's meaning, though
trying to emphasize its triviality.]

1971

D98   Anon. Review of The Doors of His Face, The Lamps
of His Mouth, and Other Stories. Kirkus Reviews,
39 (15 April), 466.
Calls Zelazny "a genial writer who somehow
manages to give old themes new twists to accomplish something bordering on the extraordinary."

D99   Anon. Review of The Doors of His Face, The Lamps
of His Mouth, and Other Stories. Publishers
Weekly, 199 (3 May), 55.
"Zelazny's ideas are clever, his delivery is
fast and glib, and he brings a southern California
style of wise-cracking hipness to perilous space."

*D100   Bischoff, D. Review of Jack of Shadows. Son of
WSFA Journal [fanzine], 39 (December), 10.
[Source: Hall.]

D101   Blish, James. Review of <u>Nine Princes in Amber</u>.
        <u>F&SF</u>, 40 (May), 39.
            Admires this work as adventure story. "The
        language is the mixture of poetry and slang char-
        acteristic of recent Zelazny, but it is not jar-
        ring here, since it makes a perfect fit with the
        hero's double life."

D102   Coulson, Robert. Review of <u>Jack of Shadows</u>.
        <u>Yandro</u> [fanzine], (October), 16.
            "Basically it's about Good and Evil and Indif-
        ference and how a man can slip from one to the
        other without realizing it."

D103   Evers, Jan M. Review of <u>The Dream Master</u>. <u>Luna</u>
        <u>Monthly</u> [fanzine], nos. 26-27 (July-August),
        pp. 46-47.
            Concentrates on book as "possible outgrowth of
        today's psychotherapy," applied to actual prac-
        tice, development of new techniques.

*D104   Hale, L. Review of <u>Creatures of Light and Dark-</u>
        <u>ness</u>. <u>Kliatt Paperback Guide</u>, 5 (February),
        Sec. 2. [Source: Hall.]

D105   Hall, H. W. Review of <u>The Doors of His Face, The</u>
        <u>Lamps of His Mouth, and Other Stories</u>. <u>Library</u>
        <u>Journal</u>, 96 (1 June), 2012.

D106   Moslander, Charlotte. Review of <u>Nine Princes in</u>
        <u>Amber</u>. <u>Luna Monthly</u> [fanzine], nos. 26-27 (July-
        August), p. 27.

*D107   Newton, J. Review of <u>Damnation Alley</u>. <u>Son of</u>
        <u>WSFA Journal</u> [fanzine], 37 (December), 9.
        [Source: Hall.]

*D108   Newton, J. Review of <u>Nine Princes in Amber</u>. <u>Son</u>
        <u>of WSFA Journal</u> [fanzine], 24 (June), 8.
        [Source: Hall.]

D109   J. J. P. [John J. Pierce]. Review of The Doors
        of His Face, The Lamps of His Mouth, and Other
        Stories. Rennaisance [fanzine], 3 (Fall), 12.
            Zelazny hero is "half proud, half cynical, al-
        ways in quest of some private grail."

D110   Robb, Alex. Review of This Immortal. SF Commen-
        tary [fanzine], no. 20 (April), pp. 28-29.
            Good on physical action. "Zelazny cannot ex-
        pose the deeper emotions, but his writing works
        by a surface razzle-dazzle." Literary borrowings
        are appropriate. An original look at immortality.

*D111   Shoemaker, M. Review of Jack of Shadows. Son of
        WSFA Journal [fanzine], 40 (December), 3.
        [Source: Hall.]

*D112   Slavin, J. Review of Nebula Award Stories Three.
        Luna Monthly [fanzine], 20 (January), 28.
        [Source: Hall.]

D113   Smith, Jeffrey D. Review of Jack of Shadows.
        Phantasmicom [fanzine], no. 8 (December),
        pp. 57-58.
            Begins as minor adventure, but shifts; last
        chapter is best part of book, as adventure is re-
        placed by morality play. Doesn't have to resolve
        physical conflict at conclusion.

D114   Smith, Jeffery D. Review of Nine Princes in
        Amber. Phantasmicom [fanzine], no. 4 (February),
        pp. 36-37.
            Corwin "a typical Zelazny near-god," but in
        best parts of novel a reader can sympathize with
        him.

D115   Waddington, Roger. Review of Creatures of Light
        and Darkness. Cypher [fanzine], no. 4 (n.d.),
        pp. 9-10.

Contains all of Zelazny's attributes, but "in an undisciplined mass." Rehash of Lord of Light without control, plot, or characterization.

1972

D116   Anon. Review of The Guns of Avalon. Kirkus Reviews, 40 (15 August), 978.
Calls Corwin "the most appealing superman since Heinlein's Valantine Michael Smith."

D117   Anon. Review of The Guns of Avalon. Publishers Weekly, 202 (28 August), 262.
"Legend retold here in a style that would curl the hair of Malory," but "Zelazny can get away with it."

D118   Bear, Greg. Review of The Doors of His Face, The Lamps of His Mouth, and Other Stories. Luna Monthly [fanzine], nos. 38-39 (July-August), p. 32.

D119   Blish, James. Review of Jack of Shadows. F&SF, 42 (April), 103-104.
Compares to Amber Series. However, Jack's motives are less comprehensible (or apparently more trivial); as opposed to consistently magical worlds, an Earth with elaborate and inconsistent machineries.

D120   Carter, Lin. Review of Jack of Shadows. Luna Monthly [fanzine], no. 34 (March), pp. 22-23.
Unsure where story is set, uncertain of rationale for action. Applauds writing but faults novel for "sloppy plotting, inadequate motivation, no background information."

D121   Chauvin, Cy, Darrell Schweitzer, Rick Stooker,
        Leon Taylor, and Murray Moore. "Hoard of Write:
        On Roger Zelazny." Prehensile [fanzine], no. 4
        (June), pp. 5-14.
            Excerpted "from a 78 page round robin [letter
        mailed from fan to fan with additions at each
        stop] run chiefly by midwestern fans." First
        section deals with Zelazny's use of myth. Taylor
        calls Zelazny sf's guru for the 1970s, represent-
        ing both "socially acceptable frivolity" and
        "socially despised honesty." Concentrates on
        Isle of the Dead, described as set not in far fu-
        ture but in slightly relabeled present. Novel is
        not successful in presenting Sandow as extraordi-
        nary, immortal god--but personable; book delivers
        less than it promises. Schweitzer: mythology in
        Isle of the Dead actually is Greek. Stooker: all
        myth/religion/fantasy "works on the same level of
        the unconscious mind." Schweitzer comments on
        Zelazny's use of myth in general. Moore compares
        the Zelazny hero to the Hemingway hero. Taylor
        agrees with Hemingway comparison but faults
        Zelazny for sloppy writing and wonders whether
        Zelazny will develop. Next section of essay con-
        siders Zelazny's prospects [less thorough than
        discussion in first section], showing general
        disappointment with Zelazny's most recent work.
        Taylor discusses weaknesses of "Eve of RUMOKO,"
        comments on peaks and valleys of Zelazny's writing
        career.

D122   Clark, Jeff. Review of Jack of Shadows. Eternity
        Science Fiction [fanzine], 1 (July), 15-17.
            "Mood is different from almost anything Zelazny
        has done before." Along with light and dark as
        plot elements in story, "a graceful somberness
        and almost a sense of tragedy." Makes fantastic
        familiar and usual strange (cf. Jack in world of
        light). Succinct but vivid descriptions.

Conclusion thwarts tragedy, as it gives incomplete
knowledge of outcome.
[Interesting extended comparison of Jack and
Corwin.]

D123   del Rey, L.   Review of Jack of Shadows.   If, 21
(February), 158-159.
Second half, without magic, "rather grim and
ugly . . . loses all the glamor it needs to be
anything but dull." As whole, rather pointless.

D124   Gillespie, Bruce.   "Something Slightly Gallant"
[review of Jack of Shadows].   SF Commentary
[fanzine], no. 26 (April), pp. 43-46.
Book seems to be tale of sword and sorcery,
but told in "clipped, precise" prose and with
logic. Style subtle, shows instead of shouting;
very well written. But story also tries to deal
with human beings: "Zelazny asks us to partici-
pate in Jack's great moral traumas, while all the
time we wish that Jack would commit a few entertaining crimes." So novel fails finally. Not
sure how morality applies in magic world.
See also letter by Jeff Clark and Gillespie's
reply, SF Commentary, no. 33 (March 1973), p. 25.

*D125   Hunter, Stephen.   "The Universe, R. Zelazny
Owner."   The Sun Magazine (Baltimore),
9 July 1972.

Phantasmicom [fanzine], no. 10 (November),
pp. 8-13 [slightly revised].
Fairly knowledgeable Sunday supplement essay,
surveying Zelazny's career, writing habits,
outlook.

D126   Marcon VII Program and Schedule Booklet.   n.p.,
n.d.
Zelazny was guest of honor. Booklet contains
brief flattering remarks by Dannie Plachta, Dean

McLaughlin, T. L. Sherred (all under one page in length), and four pages by Gordon R. Dickson, humorously introducing Zelazny to fit spy agency's specifications as ideal representative of humanity to meet freshly landed aliens.

D127   Miller, P. Schuyler. Review of The Doors of His Face, The Lamps of His Mouth, and Other Stories. Analog, 90 (September), 161-162.
    Calls title story "probably the last of the grand 'wet Venus' stories" and says "A Rose for Ecclesiastes" does same thing for traditional, romantic picture of Mars.

D128   Richey, Clarence W. Review of Nine Princes in Amber. Kliatt Paperback Guide, 6 (November), 90.
    Stresses non- (or anti-) scientific side of Zelazny's work, putting him in sword and sorcery tradition of Robert E. Howard. Also compares his work to Scott's "chivalric romances."

D129   Smith, Barbara J. Review of Jack of Shadows. Library Journal, 97 (15 January), 217.

D130   Smith, Jeffrey D. Review of The Doors of His Face, The Lamps of His Mouth, and Other Stories. Phantasmicom [fanzine], no. 10 (November), p. 62.
    Praises stories but faults their arrangements in collection.

*D131   Wadholm, Richard. Review of Jack of Shadows. Prehensile [fanzine], no. 3 (March), pp. 25-26. [Source: Mike Glyer, Prehensile's editor.]

*D132   Wadholm, R. Review of Lord of Light. Son of WSFA Journal [fanzine], 67 (September), 9-10. [Source: Hall.]

D133 Ward, Charles. Review of <u>Nine Princes in Amber</u>.
   <u>Foundation</u> [fanzine], 2 (June), 55-56.
    Zelazny's early work overpraised. Uneven, and
   overall boring. "At no time does one feel engaged with either the characters or the motiva-
   tions, for however universal vengeance or regain-
   ing of thrones may be as themes for literature,
   some kind of passion and belief must give them
   life." Zelazny condescending toward readers.
   Book feels incomplete, suffers from "lack of any
   intellectual focus."

1973

D134 Aldiss, Brian W. <u>Billion Year Spree: The True</u>
   <u>History of Science Fiction</u>. Garden City, N.Y.:
   Doubleday.
    Page 52 offers an interesting comparison be-
   tween Zelazny and Edgar Allan Poe.

D135 Anon. Review of <u>The Guns of Avalon</u>. <u>The Book-</u>
   <u>list</u>, 69 (1 January), 429.

D136 Anon. Review of <u>Jack of Shadows</u>. <u>Times Literary</u>
   <u>Supplement</u>, 3715 (18 May), 562.
    For Zelazny fans only: "this is another of
   his extravagant fables set in a quasi-medieval
   landscape of revenge and paranoia. To many the
   whole paranormal affair might seem an extraordinary mishmash of new and old literary ideas,
   couched in an inferior Morcockian [sic] prose,
   with confusion absolute."

D137 Anon. Review of <u>To Die in Italbar</u>. <u>Kirkus</u>
   <u>Reviews</u>, 41 (May), 580.
    "A slender but nicely balanced tale. . . .
   Zelazny at his not quite best is still better
   than most."

D138   Barbour, Douglas. "New Asimov/Old Zelazny" [review of The Gods Themselves (Isaac Asimov) and The Doors of His Face, The Lamps of His Mouth, and Other Stories]. Riverside Quarterly [fanzine], 6 (August), 77-78.
       Three-quarters of review devoted to Asimov. Criticizes Zelazny's choice of stories as emphasizing superficial stylistic exercises rather than longer pieces of more substance. Especially critical of omission of "For a Breath I Tarry," which "could be considered all surface, but what a sparkling, moving surface!"

D139   Carter, Lin. Imaginary Worlds: The Art of Fantasy. New York: Ballantine.
       Page 154 reports Zelazny's intention to gather/expand Dilvish stories into a book, Nine Black Doves.

*D140 D'Ammassa, D. Review of Today We Choose Faces. Son of WSFA Journal [fanzine], 94 (June), 5. [Source: Hall.]

D141   Davidson, Avram. Review of The Guns of Avalon. F&SF, 44 (April), 36-37.
       No sympathy for or interest in any of the characters or situations (had not read Nine Princes in Amber, and put off by pages of recapitulation).

D142   Fredrick, Jeremy. Review of Nine Princes in Amber and The Guns of Avalon. Son of WSFA Journal [fanzine], no. 96 (July), p. 4.

D143   Geis, Richard E. "The Case of the Blown Clone: a review of Today We Choose Faces." The Alien Critic [fanzine], no. 7 (November), p. 43.
       Rhapsodic praise. Compares to A. E. Van Vogt and Alfred Bester.

D144   Gora, Michael. "Impertinent Editorial Aside Concerning the Parentage of the Princes of Amber." Starship Tripe [fanzine], no. 5 (October), n.p.
        Brief note on apparent inconsistency in handling of Corwin's lineage.

D145   Harrison, Deborah W. Review of To Die in Italbar. Library Journal, 98 (July), 2151.

*D146   Johnson, W. Review of To Die in Italbar. Son of WSFA Journal [fanzine], 108 (October), 3. [Source: Hall.]

*D147   Livingston, D. Review of Jack of Shadows. English Journal, 5 (June), 335. [Source: Hall.]

D148   Miller, P. Schuyler. Review of To Die in Italbar. Analog, 92 (December), 167-168.
        "It isn't the best Zelazny, but it has his color and wild surmise and all the other qualities that make it impossible for him to be dull."

*D149   Miller, Steve. "Review of Today We Choose Faces." Woodwind, 5 June, p. 5. [Source: Monteleone's thesis, D150.]

D150   Monteleone, Thomas Frances. "Science Fiction as Literature: Selected Stories and Novels of Roger Zelazny." M.A. Thesis. University of Maryland.
        Utilizes Zelazny's comments on his goals and works, drawn from tape-recorded interviews: In Northrup Frye's terms, sf can form new mythology because it still uses Mythic and High Mimetic modes (pp. 12-13); also appreciated disruptive effect of Minippean satire. Monteleone considers immortality Zelazny's major theme, especially of characters in High Mimetic mode--"men of great power or ability, capable of controlling other men or combatting natural forces on even terms" (p. 25). Sees Zelazny's work as showing hunger

for life, confidence that man can cope. On importance of love: "The emotion of love, to
Zelazny, is not the romantic or courtly concept;
but instead it is a basic part of the human psyche
which can be instrumental in altering man's perceptions about himself, his environment, and his
future" (p. 27). Discusses short stories in
Chapter 2--"Passion Play," "A Rose for Ecclesiastes," "The Doors of His Face, The Lamps of His
Mouth," "Love is an Imaginary Number" [a little-
noticed story, here explicated well], "Divine
Madness," "The Keys to December," "For a Breath I
Tarry," and "The Man Who Loved the Faioli." Chapter 3 examines novels: This Immortal, The Dream
Master, and Today We Choose Faces. Discusses This
Immortal as focus of Zelazny's concern with immortality. Says Zelazny intended story as expression of Frye's High Mimetic mode, with Conrad
trying to attain stature of characters of Mythic
mode (p. 56). Other characters express some aspect of Conrad: "no matter where he turns, he
must face and confront some aspect of his own
personality. Conrad is the constant focus of the
novel since every interaction is a symbolic grap-
pling with his own complex nature" (pp. 58-59).
Richness of characters shows that immortality
need not be curse, can be always fresh and various. A search for modern myth, showing man's
hunger for gods: "The inexplicable [sic] would
remain unexplained until the power of myth gave
order to the chaos" (p. 61). Point is summed up
by Conrad and his actions. In The Dream Master,
"no one myth is examined completely or treated
with consistency. Using various myths, Zelazny
causes opposite images to shimmer, melt, and
eventually blend into each other without discor-
dance" (p. 67). In story, love is equated with
annihilation (p. 72); Render, cut off from personal feeling, believes that to care is to risk
being crushed. Ambiguous whether his choice or

his will destroys him. [For source of the ideas
and wording of this section, see D42.] In Today
We Choose Faces, hero finds he cannot remove possibility of violence without men losing something
vital. Is "evil" sometimes good? At end, hero's
and villain's consciousnesses merge, "an inver-
sion of accepted beliefs" (p. 89).

"Fire and Ice--On Roger Zelazny's Short Fiction."
Algol [fanzine], 13 (Summer 1976), 9-14.
  Based on Chapter 2 of thesis--a shortened,
tightened, updated version, discussing same
stories.

D151   Moslander, Charlotte. Review of The Guns of
        Avalon. Luna Monthly [fanzine], no. 49 (Autumn),
        p. 30.
          Comments that series is addictive, like soap
        opera.

*D152   Newton, J. Review of The Guns of Avalon. Son of
        WSFA Journal [fanzine], 82 (February), 2.
        [Source: Hall.]

D153   Ozanne, Ken. Review of The Dream Master. Son of
        WSFA Journal [fanzine], no. 110 (5 October), p. 4.

D154   Ozanne, Ken. Review of Nine Princes in Amber.
        Son of WSFA Journal [fanzine], no. 110
        (5 October), p. 4.

D155   Panshin, Alexei, and Cory Panshin. "SF in Dimen-
        sion: The Search for Mystery (1958-1967)."
        Fantastic, 22 (April), 94-113, 130.
          Discusses Zelazny and Samuel Delany as para-
        digms for sf (see D84). In discussion of This
        Immortal stresses mystery: lack of one explana-
        tion for reemergence of mythical creatures.
        "Myth is fiction that features a mystery so pow-
        erful, definite and immediate that it guides and

transforms the lives of those who encounter it.
Speculative fantasy, when it does become fully
mature, will inevitably serve this mythic func-
tion." However, Zelazny has adapted, rather than
created, myth. The Panshins call him an immature
writer, floundering since <u>Lord of Light</u>: "His
skill with language, once his most attractive
feature, has seemingly deserted him. From adapt-
ing dead myth, Zelazny has turned to inventing
dead myth, but all that his gods and heroes,
adapted or invented, seem able to do is hurl
lightning and seek revenge." For the Panshins,
Zelazny's importance is that he has led other
writers to consider mystery.

D156   Patton, B. Review of <u>The Doors of His Face, The</u>
        <u>Lamps of His Mouth, and Other Stories</u>. <u>Books and</u>
        <u>Bookmen</u>, 18 (September), 87.

D157   Pringle, David. Review of <u>Jack of Shadows</u>.
        <u>Speculation</u> [fanzine], no. 32 (March), pp. 30-32.
            Classifies as sword and sorcery: Like SF, ·
        part of Romance--"attraction is psychological
        rather than moral or intellectual. . . . Arche-
        typal themes of birth, initiation, death and re-
        birth are worked out, leaving us with a sense of
        some psychic goal attained" but without rhetoric
        of science. Instead, uses past mythology--or in-
        vented myth that tends to be sketchy and thin, as
        does Zelazny's. Novel lacks conviction in tell-
        ing, too; writing lazy, anti-climactic. Compares
        unfavorably with work of Mervyn Peake.

*D158   Ruthfork, John. "New Wave Science Fiction Con-
        sidered as a Popular Religious Phenomenon: A
        Definition and an Example." Ph.D. dissertation,
        University of New Mexico. [Source: <u>DAI</u>, 35
        (1974), 1670A-1671A.]
            Classifies Zelazny's work in three periods.
        In first, Zelazny tested how myth shapes

perception (The Dream Master) and how world without myth is chaos (This Immortal); next, explored
myths to see what meaning they could offer (Lord
of Light, Creatures of Light and Darkness);
finally, searches for meaning in almost Zen-like
coolness, sensing "timeless religious need for
meaning which can only be communicated by the
silence (Shadows) between the words of a novel."

D159   Sanders, Joe. "With Malice Toward All: A Column
About Books" [review of Jack of Shadows, Today We
Choose Faces, and Strange Doings (R. A. Lafferty)].
Starling [fanzine], no. 25 (June), pp. 12-16.
    Considers these two Zelazny novels imitative of
Jack Vance and A. E. Van Vogt respectively. World
of Jack of Shadows resembles The Dying Earth, and
elliptical characters are similar to Vance's.
However, Vance's monomaniacal heroes are easier
to understand and identify with than Zelazny's:
"Elsewhere, in Lord of Light for example, Zelazny
makes the characters part of a ritual pattern;
the echoes of symbolic roles help to flesh out the
characters. In Jack of Shadows, though, the shape
of symbolism is private." In Today We Choose
Faces, despite a deftly handled Van Vogtish plot,
characters all sound alike, so it's hard to see
how hero's attempt to change humanity has had any
effect. Overall, admits Zelazny seems confident
in what he's doing, but critic also admits own
failure to figure it out.

D160   Sturgeon, Theodore. Review of The Guns of Avalon.
Galaxy, 33 (March-April), 155.
    Dictates of sword and sorcery form unchange-
able (thus uninteresting) characters; however,
Zelazny's writing is "so cadenced and precise
and . . . characters . . . are so dimensional
that you have to love them anyway."

D161   Yoke, Carl B. "Zelazny's <u>Damnation Alley</u>:   Hell
        Noh."   <u>Extrapolation</u>, 15 (December), 6-16.
        Discusses Noh play that was added in expansion
        of magazine version.   In letter to Yoke, Zelazny
        explains as effort to show central character's
        motivation, of which he is unaware: "'A wild
        dream sequence . . . could be made to serve this
        end.'" (p. 6).   Yoke finds that besides doing
        this, the Noh play "brilliantly and succinctly
        unifies the novel . . . it focusses and deepens
        the characterization of Hell Tanner, while pro-
        viding a buoy to mark his transition from a spe-
        cific form of humanness to humanity.   In addition
        it expands and supports the novel's main theme--
        the interdependence of humanity" (p. 7).   Expli-
        cates scene largely in terms of Zelazny's
        alterations of traditional Noh forms--masks,
        costume, music, dance--to make more dramatic and
        to show Tanner reaching a kind of salvation with-
        in terms of Western religion by overcoming aliena-
        tion, becoming individual who can help others.
        [Excellent, thorough reading.]

                            1974

D162   Chauvin, Cy.   Review of <u>The Guns of Avalon</u>.
        <u>Iskra</u> [fanzine], 6 (n.d.), 37-38.
        Faults for lack of individual characteriza-
        tion, lack of serious intent.

D163   Clark, Jeff.   "What is Happening to Roger
        Zelazny?"   <u>Phantasmicom</u> [fanzine], no. 11 (May),
        pp. 60-62.
        Objects to mystery element in much of Zelazny's
        recent work, as reducing stories to superficial
        puzzles, lacking mythic power.   Discusses
        "Kjwall . . ." and <u>Today We Choose Faces</u> in most
        depth.

D164   Fowler, Christopher. Review of The Guns of
        Avalon. Cypher [fanzine], no. 12 (November),
        pp. 42-43.
            Believes Zelazny went from "humans who take on
        the aspects of gods," to characters who achieve
        larger-than-human stature while remaining mortal,
        to--in the Amber series--"beings between humans
        and gods." Finds The Guns of Avalon an advance
        over Nine Princes in Amber, since it shows Corwin
        as a more complex character, "much more of a
        fated, even a doomed, hero, somewhat in style of
        Moorcock's Elric, tortured by his own powers."
        Comments on novel's style, as altogether appro-
        priate for a character who is both inhabitant of
        twentieth-century America and a fantasy world.
        Overall, finds novel lacking the depth of which
        Zelazny is capable.

D165   Ketterer, David. New Worlds for Old: The Apoca-
        lyptic Imagination, Science Fiction, and American
        Literature. Garden City, N.Y.: Anchor [paper].
            Page 77 offers provocative comment on how
        conscious use of myth limits "displacement" in
        creation of literature.

D166   Smith, Jeff. Review of Isle of the Dead and To
        Die in Italbar. Kyben [fanzine], no. 6 (Janu-
        ary), n.p.

*D167   Swahn, Sven Christer. "Roger Zelazny." 7 x
        framtiden, Bernces förlag, Sweden, pp. 209-227.
        [Source: Carl Yoke.]

                        1975

D168   Anon. Review of Sign of the Unicorn. Booklist,
        71 (April 15), 864.

D169   Brown, Charlie. Review of <u>Sign of the Unicorn</u>.
        <u>Locus</u> [fanzine], no. 170 (March 15), p. 8.
            Can't be read independently of others in se-
        ries, but whole "is destined to be a fantasy
        classic."

D170   Burk, James K. Review of <u>Sign of the Unicorn</u>.
        <u>Delap's F&SF Review</u> [fanzine], no. 2 (May), p. 3.
            Calls Zelazny a mythmaker: "By balancing the
        god-like attributes of his protagonists with
        their very human natures, he is producing a mod-
        ern mythology." Calls attention to subtle char-
        acterization--i.e., Eric an echo of Corwin.
        Wonders whether Zelazny aware of how subtly he
        is working.

D171   Burns, Stan. Review of <u>Sign of the Unicorn</u>.
        <u>Prehensile</u> [fanzine], no. 14 (May), p. 113.

*D172   Chauvin, Cy. Review of <u>The Guns of Avalon</u>.
        <u>Amazing</u>, 48 (March), 109-110. [Source: Hall.]

D173   Davis, Monte. Review of <u>Four for Tomorrow</u>. <u>The
        Science Fiction Review Monthly</u> [fanzine], no. 10
        (December), p. 21.
            Calls stories memorable, deserving this hard-
        cover reprint (Garland). Theodore Sturgeon's
        introduction "unfortunately breathless."

*D174   Fredstrom, B. Review of <u>To Die in Italbar</u>.
        <u>Luna Monthly</u> [fanzine], 60 (December), 26.
        [Source: Hall.]

D175   Geis, Richard E. Review of <u>Sign of the Unicorn</u>.
        <u>Science Fiction Review</u> [fanzine], no. 14 (August),
        p. 34.
            "Failure as a self-contained novel," but re-
        viewer predicts "stunning conclusion to the
        saga."

D176   Gisleson, Mark. "The Effective Utilization of
        the Dastardly Bastard as Protagonist: Notes,
        Quotes, and Observations from Selected Works by
        Roger Zelazny." Unicorns & Univax [fanzine],
        no. 1 (n.d.), 1-2.
            Centers on main character who is "an anti-
        hero with whom the reader can favorably identify,
        despicable though he may be." Discusses Jack of
        Shadows, the Amber Series, Doorways in the Sand,
        Today We Choose Faces, and Damnation Alley. Dis-
        tinguishes between the genuine antihero and the
        Zelazny character, whose actions can contribute
        to personal, moral growth.

D177   "Harris, Rolf"? Review of "That Immortal." Durfed
        [fanzine], no. 1 (n.d.), p. 12.
            Parody review.

*D178   Miller, D. Review of Sign of the Unicorn.
        Panorama (Chicago Daily News), 22 March, p. 9.
        [Source: Hall.]

*D179   Morgan, C. Review of The Guns of Avalon. Victor
        [fanzine], 69 (Summer), 42-43. [Source: Hall.]

D180   Mullen, R. D. Review of Four for Tomorrow.
        Science Fiction Studies, 2 (November), 287.
            "Zelazny . . . would surely be a great success
        as a script writer for soap operas." Calls "A
        Rose for Ecclesiastes" "perhaps the best story
        ever on Mars as a dying world," but labels "The
        Doors of His Face, The Lamps of His Mouth" "per-
        haps the most turgid and cliché-ridden of all the
        retellings of Moby Dick."

D181   Mullen, R. D. Review of This Immortal. Science
        Fiction Studies, 2 (November), 287.
            Too little about future Earth or sensibilities
        of hero, though fights described in excessive
        detail.

D182   Panshin, Alexei and Cory Panshin. Review of <u>Sign of the Unicorn</u>. <u>F&SF</u>, 49 (August), 52-53, 162.
        First discusses disenchantment after Zelazny's initial reception as he wrote "one bad book after another. . . . Books in which the only reality was power and the only motive revenge. Books in which comic-book gods contended, hurling meaningless lightning at each other." Applies this description to first two Amber books and calls Zelazny inconsistent in handling details, showing hasty writing. With <u>Sign of the Unicorn</u>, though, Corwin has achieved his goals. Now can ask necessary questions, let character show some development. The Panshins also point to scene in which Corwin, wounded and hopeless, is helped by neighbor: "This man's acceptance of Corwin, complete, selfless and unquestioning, is a redemption." Praise conclusion especially, throwing away of certainties: "solipsism as a way of life is explicitly brought up and finally discarded." Zelazny called a questor, too, "launched . . . into a life-or-death improvisation . . . in honest pursuit of true reality--of whole nature and worthwhile action."
        [Impassioned but perceptive.]
        Reprinted in <u>SF in Dimension</u>. Chicago: Advent, 1976.

D183   Patton, Frederick. Review of <u>Sign of the Unicorn</u>. <u>Library Journal</u>, 100 (15 February), 412.

D184   Sherwood, Martin. Review of <u>Today We Choose Faces</u>, <u>Hard to be a God</u> (A. & B. Strugatski), <u>Ice and Iron</u> (Wilson Tucker), and <u>The California Iceberg</u> (Harry Harrison). <u>New Scientist</u>, 66 (15 May), 404-405.
        "Exercises the mind rather than befuddles it."

Part D: Critical Studies

D185   Sherwood, Martin. Review of <u>To Die in Italbar</u>,
<u>The Mote in God's Eye</u> (Larry Niven and Jerry
Pournelle), and <u>Rings of Ice</u> (Piers Anthony).
<u>New Scientist</u>, 68 (27 November), 540.
    Episodic, "less gripping than Zelazny's fast-
moving but splendidly controlled fantasies."
But "if you like jigsaw puzzles that make up into
Hieronymous Bosch pictures, you probably like all
of Zelazny."

*D186   Slater, I. Review of <u>Sign of the Unicorn</u>.
<u>Fantasie</u>, 3 (June), 7-8. [Source: Hall.]

D187   Wood, Michael. "Coffee Break for Sisyphus" [re-
view of <u>Structural Fabulation</u> (Scholes),
<u>Alternate Worlds</u> (Gunn), <u>The Dispossessed</u>
(Le Guin), and <u>Sign of the Unicorn</u>]. The
<u>New York Review of Books</u>, 22 (2 October), 3-7.
    Begins with general commentary that finds the
heart of sf to be its fascination with human
cleverness, heedlessly at work with technology or
words--creation of the story itself. Thus dubious
about claiming much serious purpose for sf, which
more often than not is escapist and gratuitous.
When finally comes to Zelazny, appreciates the
way Amber characters can manipulate physical world
at will. Also comments approvingly on style's
mixture of high-flown and colloquial language,
which Wood considers appropriate to "the brilliant
plotlessness of Zelazny's novels."

D188   Yee, Don. Review of <u>Sign of the Unicorn</u>. The
<u>Science Fiction Review Monthly</u> [fanzine], no. 1
(March), pp. 8-9.
    Calls interesting but confusing--characters,
base of family's power, etc. Praises Zelazny for
experimenting, but requests more clarity.

1976

D189   Anon. Review of <u>Bridge of Ashes</u>. <u>Publishers
       Weekly</u>, 209 (31 May), 197.

D190   Anon. Review of <u>Deus Irae</u>. <u>Publishers Weekly</u>,
       209 (2 February), 91.

D191   Anon. Review of <u>Doorways in the Sand</u>. <u>Kirkus
       Reviews</u>, 44 (15 January), 97.
           "Good natured space operetta. . . . Slight but
       snappy."

D192   Anon. Review of <u>Doorways in the Sand</u>. <u>Publishers
       Weekly</u>, 209 (2 February), 91.

D193   Anon. Review of <u>Four for Tomorrow</u>. <u>SF Booklog</u>
       [fanzine], no. 8 (March-April), p. 12.

D194   Anon. Review of <u>The Hand of Oberon</u>. <u>Publishers
       Weekly</u>, 209 (12 April), 60.

D195   Anon. Review of <u>The Hand of Oberon</u>. <u>Kirkus Re-
       views</u>, 44 (15 April), 498.
           "A series of resistible charm."

D196   Ash, Brian. <u>Who's Who in Science Fiction</u>. New
       York: Taplinger.
           Writeup on Zelazny, pp. 215-216.
           [Superficial even by encyclopedia standards.]

D197   Brodsky, Allyn B. <u>Review of My Name is Legion</u>.
       <u>The Science Fiction Review Monthly</u> [fanzine],
       no. 16 (June), pp. 6-7.
           Calls straightforward spy/detective adventure,
       but skillfully done. In such "Man vs. Problem
       stories" not much interest in characters (in fact,
       hero anti-empathetic because of callousness). Not
       first rate, but good entertainment.

D198   Brown, Charlie. Review of <u>Four for Tomorrow</u>.
       <u>Locus</u> [fanzine], no. 185 (29 February), p. 11.

D199   Burk, James K. Review of <u>Doorways in the Sand</u>.
       <u>Delap's F&SF Review</u> [fanzine], 2 (March), 4-5.
          "The fine balance of humor, mystery and adven-
       ture is kept moving at an almost breakneck pace
       by the expedient of opening most chapters with a
       'flash-forward.' This device forces the reader
       to perform some mental gymnastics and requires
       that he participate rather than merely observe."

*D200 Conan, N. Review of <u>Deus Irae</u>. <u>Science Fiction
       Review Monthly</u> [fanzine], 20 (October), 7.
       [Source: Hall.]

D201   D'Ammassa, Don. Review of <u>Bridge of Ashes</u>. <u>SF
       Booklog</u> [fanzine], no. 12 (November-December),
       pp. 2-3.
          Incredible events, no explanations. "Zelazny
       seems to be more interested in creating larger
       than life characters and conflicts of supernatural
       proportions than in reasoning out the plot."
       Calls it Zelazny's least successful novel.

D202   D'Ammassa, Don. Review of <u>Deus Irae</u>. <u>SF Booklog</u>
       [fanzine], no. 12 (November-December), p. 3.
          Doesn't represent best of either Dick or
       Zelazny. Unsure what is real, what is not; in-
       effective characters (or drawn in too much detail
       for usefulness). Styles don't mesh well; "Zelaz-
       ny's clear, short phrasing does not seem compati-
       ble with Dick's eloquent and convoluted style."

D203   D'Ammassa, Don. Review of <u>Doorways in the Sand</u>.
       <u>SF Booklog</u> [fanzine], no. 12 (November-December),
       p. 3.
          Traces of imagination but basically "a compe-
       tent, entertaining pot-boiler, and one of the
       better spy-adventure novels in the sf genre."

Cassidy's character well drawn at first but lost
in rush of action as he flounders; type of story,
"light adventure," reduces importance of character.

D204   D'Ammassa, Don. Review of <u>My Name is Legion</u>.
<u>SF Booklog</u> [fanzine], no. 12 (November-December),
p. 2.
    Better than average as formula mystery. But
"the ruthlessness of the hero, who reluctantly
but inexorably kills innocent bystanders, is
never adequately justified and may irritate some
readers."

D205   de Bolt, Joe, and John Pfeiffer. Annotated listing of <u>The Doors of His Face, The Lamps of His
Mouth and Other Stories</u>, <u>The Dream Master</u>, <u>Isle
of the Dead</u>, <u>Jack of Shadows</u>, <u>Lord of Light</u>, and
<u>This Immortal</u>. <u>Anatomy of Wonder: Science Fic-
tion</u>, ed. Neil Barron. New York: Bowker,
pp. 279-281.

D206   Doyle, C. D. Review of <u>My Name is Legion</u>. <u>Luna</u>
[fanzine], no. 66 (Winter 1976-1977), p. 43.

*D207   Freff. Review of <u>The Hand of Oberon</u>. <u>Fantasaie</u>,
4 (July), 9. [Source: Hall.]

D208   Geis, Richard E. "Faulty Structure" [review of
<u>Bridge of Ashes</u>]. <u>Science Fiction Review</u> [fan-
zine], no. 19 (November), p. 48.
    "Dennis Guise is too much the pawn in the
game, too little self-directed. The reader is
too much the observer, not enough the participant
who 'becomes' the hero."

D209   Geis, Richard E. "Lies, All Lies" [review of
<u>Deus Irae</u>]. <u>Science Fiction Review</u> [fanzine],
no. 19 (August), p. 19.

"The obvious ironic ending . . . shows the
lies that buttress and often foundation [sic] the
faiths men live by."

*D210   Goldfrank, J. Review of My Name is Legion. SF &
F Newsletter [fanzine], 15 (8 December), 3.
[Source: Hall.]

D211   Jonas, Gerald. "Of Things to Come" [review of
Doorways in the Sand, And Strange at Ecbatan the
Trees (Michael Bishop), and Antigrav (ed. Philip
Strick)]. The New York Times Book Review,
23 May, pp. 45-56.
Calls Doorways in the Sand an "entertainment"
of type written by Graham Greene. "Zelazny's
theme--whoever said that entertainment can't have
themes?--is that everyone gets the allies that he
deserves."

*D212   Jones, M. Review of My Name is Legion. Kliatt
Paperback Guide, 10 (September), 31. [Source:
Hall.]

*D213   Justice, K. Review of This Immortal. SF Booklog
[fanzine], 7 (January-February), 9. [Source:
Hall.]

D214   Last, Martin. Review of Damnation Alley. The
Science Fiction Review Monthly [fanzine], no. 15
(May), [pp. 5-6].
Finds Tanner an outdated hero, very much part
of a fixed period in U.S. history. However, description of trip "has Zelazny's typical breath-
less finesse."

D215   Last, Martin. Review of Doorways in the Sand.
The Science Fiction Review Monthly [fanzine],
no. 13 (March), [pp. 2-3].
"A deft, delicious and zany novel." Pace
keeps reader as confused as Fred, but "that's as

it should be." Zelazny's convoluted plotting
superior to Dick's because there is more interior
logic. Overcomes conventions of sf by building
impossible constructs with "conviction and tangi-
ble rationales."

D216   McPherson, W. N. Review of The Hand of Oberon.
The Science Fiction Review Monthly [fanzine],
nos. 17-18 (July-August), p. 2.
        Feels Amber series is too strung-out, requir-
ing too much summary to catch up on action, as
well as anticlimax to leave conclusion open.

D217   Meacham, Beth, and Tappan King. Review of The
Dream Master and Isle of the Dead. The Science
Fiction Review Monthly [fanzine], no. 19 (September), [pp. 16-17].
        Zelazny has one theme: "Man as Demigod fights
brave but hopeless battle against Death." Heroes
of these books are alike: world-shapers (objec-
tively or in dreams), with outstanding strength
but hubris. The Dream Master more classical ·
tragedy, "and because it abruptly leaves you to
mull its bleak conclusion, it is more resonant
reading than Dead [sic]--though not perhaps as
entertaining. In zone between sf and fantasy,
though "plausible scientific excuse" exists.
"Texture and poetry" more important than story,
since plot is so archetypal.

D218   Miller, Dan. Review of Bridge of Ashes. The
Booklist, 73 (1 October), 239.
        "En route to a flaccid finale, Zelazny often
seems to be arguing that the ends justify the
means."

D219   Miller, Dan. Review of Deus Irae. The Booklist,
73 (1 September), 23.

*D220   Miller, D.   Review of <u>Doorways in the Sand</u>.
         <u>Panorama</u> (Chicago <u>Daily News</u>), 27 March, p. 11.
         [Source: Hall.]

D221   Miller, Dan.   Review of <u>Doorways in the Sand</u>.
         <u>The Booklist</u>, 72 (1 April), 1095.
              Hero "a genuine three-dimensional character."
         "Zelazny uses his dry chuckle, superb writing,
         and a fascinating narrative to make the reader
         want to reach out and shake Cassidy's hand."

*D222   Miller, D.   Review of <u>The Hand of Oberon</u>.
         <u>Panorama</u> (Chicago <u>Daily News</u>), 22 May, p. 8.
         [Source: Hall.]

D223   Miller, Dan.   Review of <u>The Hand of Oberon</u>.   <u>The
         Booklist</u>, 73 (1 September), 24.

D224   Monteleone, Thomas F.   "Fire and Ice--On Roger
         Zelazny's Short Fiction." <u>See</u> D150.

D225   Monteleone, Thomas F.   "Introduction" to <u>Isle of
         the Dead</u>. Boston: Gregg. pp. v-xvi.
              Opens with survey of Zelazny's life and writ-
         ing career before and after writing <u>Isle of the
         Dead</u>. Stresses Zelazny's attempt to create a new
         myth, using Frye's terminology (<u>see</u> C14, D150).
         Sees Sandow as carefully constructed character in
         High Mimetic mode. Calls book "a quest tale on
         several levels" (p. x)--Sandow's surface quest,
         exploration of relationship with alien god, and
         Sandow's discovery of who he really is. Beyond
         that, says novel creates alien mythology, "a new
         archetype" (p. xi) for science fiction: a human-
         izing of technology. Culmination of Zelazny's
         fascination with mythology.

*D226   Moslander, C.   Review of <u>Sign of the Unicorn</u>.
         <u>Luna Monthly</u> [fanzine], 64 (Summer), 29.
         [Source: Hall.]

D227   Mullen, R. D. Review of <u>The Dream Master</u>. <u>Science Fiction Studies</u>, 3 (November), 303.

D228   Mullen, R. D. Review of <u>Isle of the Dead</u>. <u>Science Fiction Studies</u>, 3 (November), 303.

D229   Panshin, Alexei, and Cory Panshin. <u>SF in Dimension: A Book of Explorations</u>. Chicago: Advent.
        Several brief mentions of Zelazny but no extensive discussion, except for a reprint of D182.

D230   Parsons, Jerry L. Review of <u>The Hand of Oberon</u>. <u>Library Journal</u>, 101 (15 May), 1227.

D231   Patton, Fred. Review of <u>The Hand of Oberon</u>. <u>Delap's F&SF Review</u> [fanzine], no. 18 (September), pp. 11-12.
        Intellectually, book adds to series; emotionally feels plodding. "Zelazny is drawing it out much too long; there's not enough plot to sustain all the fine writing."

D232   Pons, Ted. Review of <u>The Hand of Oberon</u>. <u>SF Booklog</u> [fanzine], no. 12 (November-December), pp. 3-4.
        Zelazny capable of revivifying worn out genres--here, heroic fantasy. "Primary concern is tracing the development of his characters realistically through personal interaction and evolution"; thus bulk of story is intrigue, little physical conflict.

*D233   Rafalko, R. Review of <u>Deus Irae</u>. <u>Best Sellers</u>, 36 (November), 224. [Source: Hall.]

*D234   Robinson, S. Review of <u>Doorways in the Sand</u>. <u>Galaxy</u>, 37 (October), 131-132. [Source: Hall.]

D235   Seavey, Ormond. "Introduction" to <u>The Dream Master</u>. Boston: Gregg. pp. v-xii.

Describes Zelazny's perception of sf's ambivalence between view of science as Pygmalion or Frankenstein. <u>The Dream Master</u> "appears to be about a Pygmalion figure, a life-giving artist. It proves in the end to be about a half-deluded scientist, a Frankenstein." Discusses Zelazny's allusions to myths, names. Technology blurs distinctions: "Man and machine, man and beast, God and man, illusion and reality--all seem to be not opposing states but merely alternative modes of perception." Discusses sf as product/cause of fantasy. Put off by Zelazny's humor, considers it an aspect of writing for subculture. Zelazny's personal confidence reflected in characters, who tend to be interchangeably brash, daring, and attractive; even in "The Doors of His Face, The Lamps of His Mouth" "there are no Moby Dicks in Zelazny's fiction, nothing outside the self which offers insuperable obstacle." Render is typical of Zelazny's heroes in confidence--but shows limitations of this confidence when blind to own vulnerability. Blindness one of novel's themes, as Render lapses into private fantasy (opposite of myth).

D236   Shippey, T. A. Review of <u>To Die in Italbar</u>. <u>Times Literary Supplement</u>, 3858 (20 February), 187.

"Mr. Zelazny relies heavily on his ability to suggest the presence in the background of whole worlds and policies and technologies, all profoundly interesting but too large for comprehension. It is almost a pity that the convention of the novel forces a plot and an ending on him."

*D237   Siciliano, Sam Joseph. "The Fictional Universe in Four Science Fiction Novels." Ph.D. dissertation, University of Iowa. [Source: DAI, 36 (1976), 8053A.]

    Discusses <u>Creatures of Light and Darkness</u> as unexplained mystery, between ironic and heroic in tone, giving reader experience of the fantastic.

D238   Sisco, E. Review of <u>Doorways in the Sand</u>. <u>School Library Journal</u>, 23 (October), 124.

*D239   Stephensen-Payne, P. Review of <u>Today We Choose Faces</u>. <u>Vector</u> [fanzine], 72 (February), 38. [Source: Hall.]

*D240   Walkoff, L. Review of <u>The Hand of Oberon</u>. <u>Best Sellers</u>, 36 (September), 188. [Source: Hall.]

D241   Weiner, Paula J. Review of <u>Doorways in the Sand</u>. <u>Library Journal</u>, 101 (15 March), 837.

D242   Wood, Susan. Review of <u>Doorways in the Sand</u>. <u>Locus</u> [fanzine], no. 184 (31 January), pp. 5, 7.

    Suggests Zelazny deserves fresh evaluation after post-debut letdown. This novel better than average, but not up to Zelazny's potential--especially since Zelazny's writing goes beyond merely functional through literary allusions, clever lines, pretentious passages. Critical of first person narrator form, "since the narrator has to be used to tell his . . . own story, give us a sense of his personality, suggest enough of outside events and responses to give another perspective on that character. Over and over in his work, Zelazny only accomplishes the first of these tasks. ('A Rose for Ecclesiastes' is a notable exception.)" Hero is nonentity, unconvincing but entertaining.

D243   Wood, Susan. Review of <u>My Name is Legion</u>.
        <u>Delap's F&SF Review</u> [fanzine], no. 15 (June),
        pp. 17-18.
            Catches biblical reference in title to "un-
        clean spirit," but sees hero's regret for suffer-
        ing he causes. Especially fond of third novella,
        "Home is the Hangman," as vivid and meaningful
        work, as good as Zelazny of the 1960s.

                            1977

*D244   Adams, R. Review of <u>Doorways in the Sand</u>.
        <u>Kliatt Young Adult Paperback Book Guide</u>, 11
        (Spring), 13. [Source: Hall.]

D245   Brown, Charles N. Review of <u>My Name is Legion</u>.
        <u>Isaac Asimov's Science Fiction Magazine</u>, 1
        (Spring), 149.

*D246   Budrys, A. Review of <u>Doorways in the Sand</u>.
        <u>F&SF</u>, 53 (July), 107. [Source: Hall.]

*D247   Caimmi, Giuseppe, and Piergiorgio Nicolzzini.
        "Ritratto di Roger Zelazny." <u>Robot 10: Rivista
        di fantascienza</u>, Armenia Editore, Milan, Italy.
        [Source: Carl Yoke.]

D248   Cowper, Richard. "A Rose is a Rose is a
        Rose . . . in Search of Roger Zelazny."
        <u>Foundation</u>, nos. 11-12 (March), pp. 142-147.
            Personal meditation on dissatisfaction with
        Zelazny's most recent work, especially in light
        of earlier ecstatic responses. In particular,
        contrasts "A Rose for Ecclesiastes" with <u>To Die
        in Italbar</u>. Compares Zelazny to Byron in "for-
        midable creative energy" and "commensurate lack
        of creative discipline." Criticizes <u>To Die in
        Italbar</u> for cliché-stuffed style, incredible
        characterization--narrative force used as

"substitute for psychological subtlety." Style is dazzling but undisciplined, subject to frequent lapses. Finds hope in Doorways in the Sand, though still not fulfilling Zelazny's early promise.

D249   Delany, Samuel R. The Jewel-Hinged Jaw: Notes on the Language of Science Fiction. Elizabethtown, N.Y.: Dragon Press. See D57.

*D250   del Rey, L. Review of Bridge of Ashes. Analog, 97 (January), 172-173. [Source: Hall].

D251   Fredericks, S. C. "Revivals of Ancient Mythologies in Current Science Fiction and Fantasy." In Many Futures, Many Worlds: Theme and Form in Science Fiction, ed. Thomas D. Clareson. Kent, Ohio: Kent State University Press, pp. 50-65.
     Discusses Zelazny's revival of entire ancient mythologies "with detailed correspondence in characters, theme, and atmosphere" (p. 52). Examines This Immortal, Lord of Light (in which, reversing Christian redemption, gods must be made into men), and Creatures of Light and Darkness [a very lucid plot summary].

D252   Geis, Richard. Review of Doorways in the Sand. Science Fiction Review [fanzine], no. 21 (May), p. 16.
     "Too tongue-in-cheek."

D253   Geis, Richard. Review of Nine Princes in Amber. Science Fiction Review [fanzine], no. 21 (May), p. 57.

D254   Glyer, Mike. "The Six Who are Boring." Scientifriction [fanzine], no. 9 (November), pp. 5-7.
     Parody anticipating conclusion of Amber series.

Part D: Critical Studies

*D255   Haines, L. Review of <u>Sign of the Unicorn</u>.
<u>Kliatt Young Adult Paperback Book Guide</u>, 11
(Winter), 10. [Source: Hall.]

D256   Hooks, Wayne. Review of <u>Damnation Alley</u>.
<u>Delap's F&SF Book Review</u> [fanzine], 3 (March),
30-31.
    Action underdeveloped, rushed. Tanner a
dated, stereotyped character, inconsistent and
lacking real motivation: "a mild adventure with
an easily foreseeable conclusion, utilizing an
abbreviated pilgrimage motif. There are no deep
meanings here."

*D257   Lewis, S. Review of <u>Bridge of Ashes</u>. <u>Science
Fiction Newsletter</u> [fanzine], 18 (21 February),
3-4. [Source: Hall.]

*D258   Morgan, C. Review of <u>Sign of the Unicorn</u>.
<u>Vector</u> [fanzine], 81 (May-June), 18. [Source:
Hall.]

D259   Murn, Thomas J. "Irresistable [sic] Schlog Meets
Immovable Critic" [review of <u>Bridge of Ashes</u> and
<u>Doorways in the Sand</u>]. <u>Janus</u> [fanzine], 3
(n.d.), 58.
    Zelazny is working within adventure sf conven-
tions, but trying to raise them to more mature
level.

*D260   Robinson, S. Review of <u>My Name is Legion</u>.
<u>Galaxy</u>, 38 (May), 145-146. [Source: Hall.]

D261   Sanders, Joe. Review of <u>Deus Irae</u>. <u>Delap's F&SF
Review</u> [fanzine], no. 23 (February), pp. 17-18.
    Guesses what each author contributed. Finds
change of direction, from Dick's anxious indeci-
sion to Zelazny's breezy action, too jarring; un-
prepared for conclusion.

D262   Schweitzer, Darrell. Review of <u>The Dream Master</u>. <u>Science Fiction Review</u> [fanzine], no. 20 (February), p. 35.
"His best, and one of the all-time great science fiction novels."

D263   Stableford, Brian M. "A Mazing Grace" [review of <u>The Hand of Oberon</u> and <u>Bridge of Ashes</u>]. <u>Foundation</u>, nos. 11–12 (March), pp. 148–150.
Questions whether these stories are truly complete, despite length. Voices suspicion that Amber series could be endless, as already built pattern repeatedly is torn down, new characters constantly emerge. On <u>Bridge of Ashes</u>, comments on plot skeleton's lack of connective tissue: "around the few jigsaw pieces the reader is privileged to experience there is a great wilderness of ignorance which may only be mapped by conjecture." Discusses incompleteness as policy in Zelazny's work, giving vigorous pace and obscuring inconsistencies and trivialities. Says such style is characteristic of short stories,. shouting to grab reader's attention. Zelazny is sf's "most brilliant . . . exponent of these techniques"; in sf, they substitute for formal realism and characterization, the stuff of whole novels.

D264   Stewart, Duane. "The Corridors of Her Esophagus, The Headlights of Her Eyes." <u>Yandro</u> [fanzine], no. 240 (July), pp. 9–12.
Parody of Zelazny's sword and sorcery: Dilvish stories (especially "A Knight for Merytha)," <u>Jack of Shadows</u>, and the Amber series.

D265   Vardeman, Bob. "This Immortal (talent)--Roger Zelazny." <u>MileHiCon #9 Program Booklet</u>, 20–30 October, pp. 7–9.
Brief appreciation, with list of nominations and awards.

D266   Watson, Jay W.   Review of <u>Isle of the Dead</u>.
        <u>Delap's F&SF Review</u> [fanzine], no. 22 (January),
        pp. 25-26.

D267   Wood, Susan.   Review of <u>Bridge of Ashes</u>.   <u>Delap's</u>
        <u>F&SF Review</u> [fanzine], no. 27 (June), pp. 35-36.
            On conclusion: "For perhaps three pages, the
        Zelazny talent flashes out, in service of a plot
        both arbitrary and unconvincing."   Characteriza-
        tions underdeveloped; in particular, "the poten-
        tial focus of the book, Dennis Guise's own
        reactions are never really explored."

                        1978

D268   Anon.   Review of <u>The Courts of Chaos</u>.   <u>Kirkus</u>
        <u>Reviews</u>, 46 (15 August), 906.
            "Often clever and thoughtful writer, Zelazny
        here is an anything-goes artist who slaps together
        Yeatsian imagery and paradoxes of cause and iden-
        tity with the aid of a perfunctorily realized
        fantasy-landscape and a style of jarring unpre-
        dictability.   Admirers of the series profess to
        find in it all sorts of Jungian resonances and
        manipulation of witty incongruities.   The rest of
        us will be rather relieved to see it end."

D269   Anon.   Review of <u>The Courts of Chaos</u>.   <u>Publishers</u>
        <u>Weekly</u>, 214 (7 August), 68.
            "Zelazny deserves credit for his grand vision,
        yet somehow the result, though entertaining,
        falls short of the excitement one would have
        hoped to find in this climactic novel--perhaps
        because so much of the action is subjective."

*D270   Anon.   Review of <u>Doorways in the Sand</u>.   <u>Observer</u>
        [London], 1 January, p. 33.   [Source: <u>Book Re-</u>
        <u>view Index</u>.]

D271   Brown, Charles N. Review of <u>The Courts of Chaos</u>.
        <u>Isaac Asimov's Science Fiction Magazine</u>, 2 (May-
        June), 12-13.

*D272   Corley, J. Review of <u>The Hand of Oberon</u>. <u>Vector</u>
        [fanzine], 86 (May-April), 34-36. [Source:
        Hall.]

*D273   Corley, J. Review of <u>Lord of Light</u>. <u>Vector</u>
        [fanzine], 86 (May-April), 34-36. [Source:
        Hall.]

 D274   de Jonge, Alex. Review of <u>The Hand of Oberon</u>.
        <u>Spectator</u>, 240 (1 April), 24.
            Links to wave of lumbering mock-epics imitat-
        ing Tolkien; considers a waste of Zelazny's
        talent.

 D275   Emerson, David. Review of <u>The Courts of Chaos</u>.
        <u>Locus</u> [fanzine], no. 216 (November), p. 7.
            Considering huge number of questions left un-
        answered in earlier Amber books, "all the remain-
        ing unknowns of the plot are answered, but in a
        rather didactic manner . . . and the major [back-
        ground] questions are left unanswered." Plenty
        of action thrown in, but still a desultory let-
        down. "The one hopeful note is that Zelazny has
        left himself an out: <u>this</u> story may be over, but
        there's a whole new universe . . . and Corwin is
        once more footloose and ready for adventure."

*D276   Miller, D. Review of <u>The Courts of Chaos</u>. <u>Book-
        list</u>, 5 (1 December), 604. [Source: Hall.]

*D277   Miller, D. Review of <u>The Illustrated Roger
        Zelazny</u>. <u>Booklist</u>, 74 (1 June), 1539-1540.
        [Source: Hall.]

*D278   Parsons, J. Review of <u>The Courts of Chaos</u>.
        <u>Library Journal</u>, 103 (1 October), 2010. [Source:
        Hall.]

 D279   Robinson, Spider. Review of <u>The Illustrated</u>
        <u>Roger Zelazny</u>. <u>Analog</u>, 98 (September), 169-172.
            Discusses book as part of evolution of
        illustration/comic art.

 D280   Sanders, Joe. Review of <u>The Courts of Chaos</u>.
        <u>The Lakeland Forum</u>, no. 1 (Spring), pp. 26-27.

*D281   Walker, Paul. <u>Speaking of Science Fiction</u>. New
        York: LUNA Publications.
            <u>See</u> C35.

*D282   Weston, J. Review of <u>Doorways in the Sand</u>. <u>New</u>
        <u>Scientist</u>, 1091 (23 February), 520. [Source:
        Hall.]

 D283   Wolkoff, Lew. Review of <u>The Illustrated Roger</u>
        <u>Zelazny</u>. <u>Best Sellers</u>, 38 (June), 73.

                                1979

 D284   Ackerman, Forrest J. "Zelazny Strikes Again"
        [cf. contents page--on actual page labeled
        "Coming Attractions: Futuria Fantasia Film
        Flashes"]. <u>Famous Monsters</u>, no. 157 (September),
        pp. 23-24.
            Covers Zelazny's books under film options.

 D285   Barbour, Douglas. "The Doors of His Face, The
        Lamps of His Mouth, and Other Stories." In
        <u>Survey of Science Fiction Literature</u>, ed. Frank N.
        Magill. Vol. 2. Englewood Cliffs, N.J.: Salem
        Press, pp. 583-586.

D286   Carper, Steve.   Review of <u>The Courts of Chaos</u>.
        <u>Science Fiction & Fantasy Book Review</u>, 1 (March),
        16.
            "There are a few surprises, some nice flashes
        of maturity in the generally unlikable and self-
        indulgent gods who serve as protagonists, and a
        general air of weariness about the whole con-
        cept." Hopes Zelazny is capable of recapturing
        earlier brilliance.

D287   CNB [Charles N. Brown].   Review of <u>Roadmarks</u>.
        <u>Locus</u>, no. 227 (November), p. 18.
            "Reads more like an outline than . . . com-
        pleted book."

D288   Currey, L. W.   Entry on Zelazny in <u>Science Fic-
        tion and Fantasy Authors: A Bibliography of
        First Printings of Their Science Fiction and
        Selected Nonfiction</u>.   Boston: G. K. Hall.
            Pages 570-571 provide a bibliographical check-
        list of first and selected later printings and
        editions of Zelazny's books through December 1977
        with emphasis on points for identification.

D289   JC [John Clute].   Entry on Zelazny in <u>The Science
        Fiction Encyclopedia</u>, ed. Peter Nicholls.   Garden
        City, N.Y.:   Doubleday.
            Pages 671-672 review Zelazny's career, with
        commentary on specific works, such as this remark
        on <u>The Dream Master</u>:   "Throughout his career RZ
        [sic] has a tendency to side, perhaps a little
        too openly, with his complexly gifted, vain,
        dominating protagonists."   Critical of recent
        work, but hopeful of rebirth.

D290   Mayo, Clark.   "This Immortal."   In <u>Survey of
        Science Fiction Literature</u>, ed. Frank N. Magill.
        Vol. 5.   Englewood Cliffs, N.J.:   Salem Press,
        pp. 2260-2263.

D291   Parsons, Jerry L. Review of The Illustrated
        Roger Zelazny. Science Fiction & Fantasy Book
        Review, 1 (April), 34.

D292   Sanders, Joe. Review of The Courts of Chaos.
        Science Fiction & Fantasy Book Review, 1 (March),
        16-17.
            Calls the Amber series "the best sword and
        sorcery story in years--maybe ever." Delighted
        by Zelazny's giving fresh, human concern to a
        form that seemed fit only for shallow wish ful-
        fillment. "Against all odds, extravagantly and
        beautifully, Amber does matter."

D293   Sanders, Joe. Review of The Illustrated Roger
        Zelazny. Science Fiction & Fantasy Book Review,
        1 (August), 98.

D294   Sanders, Joe. "Zelazny: Unfinished Business."
        In Voices for the Future: Essays on Major Science
        Fiction Writers, Volume Two. Bowling Green, Ohio:
        Bowling Green University Popular Press, pp. 180-
        196.
            Survey of Zelazny's career, stressing style
        and theme: open-ended form displays confidence
        in characters' abilities to grow. Discusses sev-
        eral stories in passing, including "Horseman!,"
        "Passion Play," "A Museum Piece," "A Rose for
        Ecclesiastes" (explication of Gallinger's growth,
        seeing story's conclusion as hopeful), "For a
        Breath I Tarry." Of novels, spends most time on
        This Immortal and Lord of Light; in latter con-
        trasts Sam with Deicrats, the party of stability
        and fixed religious values: "Trying to preserve
        a static, peaceful society, they organize in-
        creasingly cataclysmic battles. Their accomplish-
        ment, finally, is folly. Sam does not take him-
        self so seriously . . . but he practices more
        wisdom. He is not sure exactly who he is or what
        he can do; however, he is free to improvise

brilliantly on new opportunities and new abili-
ties he finds in himself. The novel's overall
action demonstrates the deadly sterility of re-
fusing to change, and the ultimate viability of
accepting natural growth. Sam's way finally
works" (p. 192). Rushes through later works,
with some space for Doorways in the Sand.

D295   Schweitzer, Darrell. Review of Today We Choose
Faces. Thrust--Science Fiction in Review, no. 12
(Summer), pp. 39-40.
    Sees "Zelazny shifting gears," away from
"overt use of mythology." Comments on protago-
nist's confusion and wonders whether Zelazny was
fully in control of story; however, praises vivid
writing and good movement from scene to scene.

D296   Thurston, Robert. "Introduction" to Today We
Choose Faces. Boston: Gregg, pp. v-xix.
    Emphasizes, in Zelazny's work as a whole, the
practice of "breaking reality into pieces, throw-
ing bricks through windows of structures that
comfortably house the traditional patterns of
thought. . . . His characters are often faced
with the problem of assembling the fragments,
the bits and pieces of life, that are either
obstacles to their overall quests or clues which
will guide them toward their important destinies"
(pp. v-vi). Discusses religious themes, such as
the nature of good and evil and man's relationship to God (though stressing that the novel is
not written to preach a Christian message). Relates specific passages to Dante's Inferno.
Detailed explication of confrontation between
di Negri (violence, evil) and Styler (reason,
good), showing also that Styler addresses di Negri
in evolving terms of worshiper confronting silent
god. In bulk of book, di Negri directly takes
over role of god, to reshape man as rational and
nonviolent. But this is shaken apart by end of

story, as attitude returns to opening's uncertainty--however, this time accepting it: "uncertainty is always the right answer to the question of man's relationship to his god, as well as to the question of his role in the universe. But man must proceed on to the next new idea, or renewal of an old one, to see how it affects traditional patterns of thought and/or transfigures reality and humankind" (p. xvi). Also compares work to detective story form, to Hamlet, and to Oedipus Rex, concluding that Zelazny is not only daring in attempting to put so many different things together but successful in making connections that integrate all into a new whole.

D297   Wilcox, Robert H. "Between the Lines." Fantastic, 27 (July), 77-79.
       Accompanies reprint of "A Museum Piece."

D298   Wooster, Martin Morse. Review of The Courts of Chaos. Thrust--Science Fiction in Review, no. 13 (Fall), pp. 42, 44.
       "Zelazny has written a fairly good novel, if not the masterpiece his supporters were hoping for." Actually comments on the whole series. "Zelazny is once again playing with his favourite subject--alienated gods able to control the universe, but unable to act, brooding Hamlets poised on the brink."

D299   Yoke, Carl. "The Dream Master." In Survey of Science Fiction Literature, ed. Frank N. Magill. Vol. 2. Englewood Cliffs, New Jersey: Salem Press, pp. 608-613.

D300   Yoke, Carl. "Lord of Light." In Survey of Science Fiction Literature, ed. Frank N. Magill. Vol. 3. Englewood Cliffs, New Jersey: Salem Press, pp. 1251-1256.

D301 Yoke, Carl. <u>A Reader's Guide to Roger Zelazny</u>.
West Linn, Oregon: Starmont House [paper].
Goes beyond literary analysis to show sources
of themes and ideas in Zelazny's work, especially
Zelazny's long-standing philosophy of necessary
interaction of form and chaos. Discusses major
works in separate chapters. For "A Rose for
Ecclesiastes" explicates both parts of title--
Rose (Braxa) a symbol of transformation; Ecclesiastes represents pessimism (Martians) and
condemnation of vanity (in experience of
Gallinger). Gallinger is transformed by love.
"He has learned humility. Though he has justified his vanity up to this point by rationalizing
it with the acclaim he has received on Earth for
his genius, the experience of love has forced his
maturity" (p. 23). Yoke states that <u>This Immortal</u>
also focuses on renewal, beginning with the link-
ing of Conrad to figures of mythic stature, especially to "dying and reviving gods" (cf. Sir
James G. Frazer and Jesse Weston's <u>From Ritual to
Romance</u>). Links "The Doors of His Face, The Lamps
of His Mouth" to Book of Job in concept of Levi-
athan and stress on need to overcome pride. Reads
<u>The Dream Master</u> in terms of Jung's theory of re-
treat from unsatisfying world into unconscious;
myths of Tristram and Isolde (considered an unfortunate choice of Zelazny's, since many varia-
tions of myth confuse interpretation), myth of
<u>ragnarok</u>. Shows how <u>Lord of Light</u> uses contrast
between Hinduism and Buddhism to demonstrate that
stagnant society must be torn down and leads to
discussion of Zelazny's belief that both chaos
and form are necessary parts of life. Explains
"Home is the Hangman" in terms of abuse of tech-
nology--yet recognizing possibility of unexpected
application: "Ultimately, the Hangman is an example of how man--even with his bumbling, greed,
often limited perception, brashness, immaturity
and lack of wisdom--somehow manages to extend

himself" (p. 79). Discusses Amber series as whole; believes main achievement is successful showing of how Corwin changes through experience. Traces Grail motifs, cf. Jesse Weston. Concludes with a chapter summarizing plots of other major works.

[Besides perceptive reading and familiarity with myth and psychology, Yoke can draw on a thirty-year friendship with Zelazny, referring to conversations and letters. An excellent study.]

D302   Yoke, Carl. <u>Roger Zelazny and Andre Norton:</u> <u>Proponents of Individualism</u>. Columbus, Ohio: The State Library of Ohio [paper].

Missing: Fanzine reviews in <u>WSFA Journal</u>, no. 70, mention a "comprehensive" essay on Zelazny in <u>Forum International</u>, no. 1, July 1969, published by the Scandinavian Science Fiction Society.

Around 1969, <u>WSFA Journal</u> published a bibliography of Zelazny's fanzine appearances (source: Mark Owings, confirmed by Zelazny). I assume this was the same bibliography noted among the manuscripts at Syracuse University (<u>see</u> Appendix C) and mailed to me by Zelazny. As such, it has been incorporated in this work. However, I have been unable to check the published bibliography itself--or to see what additions and corrections readers might have contributed.

Appendixes

A: Nominations, Awards, and Honors

Information sources: Bob Vardeman (D264), Carl Yoke, Zelazny's vitae, and Locus.

1964 "A Rose for Ecclesiastes"--Hugo nomination

1965 "He Who Shapes"--won Nebula (novella)
"The Doors of His Face, The Lamps of His Mouth"--
won Nebula (novelette)
"Devil Car"--Nebula nomination (short story)

1966 "This Moment of the Story"--Nebula nomination
(novelette)
"The Doors of His Face, The Lamps of His Mouth"--
Hugo nomination (novelette)
"An Call Me Conrad"--won Hugo (novel)

1967 "Comes Now the Power"--Hugo nominatiin (short
story)
"This Mortal Mountain"--Hugo nomination (short
story)
"For a Breath I Tarry"--Hugo nomination
(novelette)
"This Moment of the Storm"--Hugo nomination
(novelette)
"The Keys to December"--Nebula nomination
(novelette)
Lord of Light--Nebula nomination (novel)

1968 "Damnation Alley"--Hugo nomination (novella)
   Lord of Light--won Hugo (novel)
   "A Rose for Ecclesiastes"--voted by Science Fic-
    tion Writers of America as one of top fifteen
    stories ever written (sixth place); as such,
    included in The Science Fiction Hall of Fame
    (see A24)

1969 Isle of the Dead--Nebula nomination (novel)

1972 Jack of Shadows--Hugo nomination (novel)
   Isle of the Dead--won Prix Apollo (French)

1974 "The Engine at Heartspring's Center"--Nebula
    nomination (short story)

1975 "The Engine at Heartspring's Center"--Jupiter
    nomination (short story)
   "Home is the Hangman"--won Nebula (novella)
   Doorways in the Sand--Nebula nomination (novel)

1976 "Home is the Hangman"--won Hugo (novella)
   Doorways in the Sand--Hugo nomination (novel)

1977 Doorways in the Sand--selected by the American
    Library Association as one of the Best Books
    for Young Adults published in 1976
   The Hand of Oberon--Ditmar (Australian) nomina-
    tion (novel)

1979 Zelazny nominated for Galdalf Award for Grand
    Master of Fantasy

B: Foreign Language Editions

In most cases, foreign language editions have been omitted from the body of this bibliography. However, they are a useful indication of Zelazny's growing reputation world-wide--and in the case of the French edition of Isle of the Dead, a translation won Zelazny one of his major awards.

Only books are listed in this section. It is prohibitively difficult to trace all the reprintings of individual stories. Not even Zelazny keeps track of these. This list is based on the author's copies of foreign editions actually received by Zelazny.

Dutch

Noem me maar Conrad. Utrecht/Antwerp: Uitgegeverij
    Het Spectrum, 1970 [paper].
Heer van het Licht [Lord of Light]. Utrecht/
    Antwerp: Uitgegeverij Het Spectrum, 1972 [paper].
Een Roos voor de Prediker. Utrecht/Antwerp:
    Uitgegeverij Het Spectrum, 1972 [paper].
Jack van de Schaduwen. Utrecht/Antwerp: Uit-
    gegeverij Het Spectrum, 1973 [paper].
Hellevart [Damnation Alley]. Utrecht/Antwerp:
    Uitgegeverij Het Spectrum, 1974 [paper].
Prinsen van Amber. Utrecht/Antwerp: Uitgegeverij
    Het Spectrum, 1974 [paper].
De Weg naar Amber. Utrecht/Antwerp: Uitgegeverij
    Het Spectrum, 1974 [paper].

Sterven in Italbar. Utrecht/Antwerp: Uitgegeverij
    Het Spectrum, 1975 [paper].
De hand van Oberon. Utrecht/Antwerp: Uitgegeverij
    Het Spectrum, 1977 [paper].
Kindern van de aarde [Bridge of Ashes]. Utrecht/
    Antwerp: Uitgegeverij Het Spectrum, 1977 [paper].
Mijn nam is Legioen. Utrecht/Antwerp: Uitgegeverij
    Het Spectrum, 1977 [paper].
Stersteen [Doorways in the Sand]. Utrecht/Antwerp:
    Uitgegeverij Het Spectrum, 1977 [paper].
Het ware Amber [Sign of the Unicorn]. Utrecht/
    Antwerp: Uitgegeverij Het Spectrum, 1978 [paper].
De hoven van Chaos. Utrecht/Antwerp: Uitgegeverij
    Het Spectrum, 1979 [paper].

French

L'îsle des Mortes. Paris: Editions OPTA, 1971
    [paper]; this edition succeeded by Paris: J'ai
    Lu, n.d. [paper].
Royaumes d'ombre et de Lumière. Paris: Editions
    Denöel, 1972 [paper].
Toi, L'Immortal. Paris: Editions Denoël, 1973
    [paper].
Les Culbateurs de L'Enfer [Damnation Alley]. Paris:
    Chute Libre, 1974 [paper].
Seigneur de Lumière. Paris: Editions Denoël, 1974
    [paper].
Les 9 Princes D'Ambre. Paris: Editions Denoël,
    1975 [paper].
Les Fusils D'Avalon. Paris: Editions Denoël, 1976
    [paper].
Le Sérum de la Déesse bleue [To Die in Italbar].
    Paris: Editions Denoël, 1976 [paper].
Aujourd'hui Nous Changeons de Visage [Today We
    Choose Faces]. Paris: Editions Denoël, 1977
    [paper].
Le Maître des Rêves. Paris: Casterman, 1977
    [paper].

Le Signe de la Licorne. Paris: Editions Denoël,
   1978 [paper].
L'Homme qui N'existait Pas [My Name is Legion].
   Paris: Presses Pocket, 1978 [paper].
La main d'Oberon. Paris: Editions Denoël, 1979
   [paper].
Les culbateurs de l'enfer [Damnation Alley]. Paris:
   Titres SF, 1974 [paper].

German

   Strasse der Verdammnis. Munich: Wilhelm Heyne
      Verlag, 1972 [paper].
   Fluch der Unsterblichkeit [This Immortal]. Hamburg/
      Dusseldorf: Marion von Schröder Verlag, 1973;
      Rastatt/Baden: Erich Pabel Verlag, n.d. [paper].
   Die Insel der Toten. Munich: Wilhelm Heyne Verlag,
      1973 [paper].
   Die Türen seines Gesichts, die Lampen seines
      Mundes. . . . Munich: Konig Verlag, 1973 [paper].
   Heut wählen wir Gesichter. Munich: Wilhelm Heyne
      Verlag, 1975 [paper].
   Der Tod in Italbar. Munich: Wilhelm Heyne Verlag,
      1975 [paper].
   Herr des Lichtes. Munich: Wilhelm Heyne Verlag,
      1976 [paper].
   Corwin von Amber. Munich: Wilhelm Heyne Verlag,
      1977 [paper].
   Die Gewehre von Avalon. Munich: Wilhelm Heyne
      Verlag, 1977 [paper].
   Im Zeichen des Einhorns. Munich: Wilhelm Heyne
      Verlag, 1977 [paper].
   Die Aschenbrücke [Bridge of Ashes]. Munich:
      Wilhelm Heyne Verlag, 1978 [paper].
   Die Hand Oberons. Munich: Wilhelm Heyne Verlag,
      1978 [paper].

Greek

ΕΠΙΣΤΡΟΦΗ ΣΤΗ ΓΗ [This Immortal]. Athens:
Ekdoeseis Epsilon, n.d. [probably published in
late 1968 or early 1969--Zelazny] [paper].

Hebrew

אדון האור [Lord of Light]. Tel Aviv: Am Oved,
1978 [paper].

Italian

Io, L'Immortale. Piacenza: Casa Editrice La Tri-
buna, 1971 [paper].
Signore de Sogni [The Dream Master]. Piacenza:
Casa Editrice La Tribuna, 1971 [paper].
Metamorfosi Cosmica [Isle of the Dead]. Milan:
Editrice Nord, 1974.
Creature della Luce e della Tenebre. Turin: Casa
Editrice MEB, 1975 [paper].
Jack delle Ombre. Milan: Longanesi & Co., 1975
[paper].
Signore Della Luce. N.p.: Casa Editrice Nord, 1975.
Morire a Italbar. Milan: Longanesi & Co., 1977
[paper].
Scegli Un Nuovo Volto. Milan: Longanesi & Co.,
1977 [paper].
Nove Principi in Ambra. Bologna: Libra Editrice,
1978.
Le Armi di Avalon. Bologna: Libra Editrice, 1979.
La Piota dell'orrore [Damnation Alley]. Milan:
Arnoldo Mondadori, 1979 [paper].

Japanese

Damnation Alley. Tokyo: Hayakawa-Shobo & Co., Ltd.,
1972 [paper].
Lord of Light. Tokyo: Hayakawa-Shobo & Co., Ltd.,
1975 [paper].

The Doors of His Face, The Lamps of His Mouth, And
Other Stories. Tokyo: Hayakawa Publishing Co.,
1976 [paper].
Nine Princes in Amber. Tokyo: Hayakawa, 1979
[paper].

Spanish

Una Rosa para el Eclesiastés. Buenos Aires,
Argentina: Editorial Sudamericana, 1974 [paper].
Tú, el immortal. Barcelona: Ediciones Martinez
Roca, S.A., 1977 [paper].
El hombre que no existia [My Name is Legion].
Buenos Aires: Editorial Sudamericana, 1978
[paper].
El Señor de la Luz [Lord of Light]. Buenos Aires:
Ediciones Mirotauro, 1979 [paper].

Swedish

Skuggornas Herre [Jack of Shadows]. N.p.: Bernces
forlag, 1974 [paper].

C: Manuscripts and Papers

Students of Zelazny are fortunate that his writing
career has coincided with growing academic interest in
sf. As a consquence, the bulk of Zelazny's manuscripts
and public papers are available for study in two large
collections: at the George Arents Research Library at
Syracuse University, and at the University of Maryland,
Baltimore County.

I. The Roger Zelazny Papers, George Arents Research
Library at Syracuse University

The following description of the papers was written
by the staff of the George Arents Research Library.
Zelazny material and manuscripts are probably to be
found in other collections at Syracuse, including those
from Mercury Press and Galaxy. Note that the material
is stored in separate, numbered boxes. A librarian has
attempted to categorize the material before dividing it
for storage. I have added quotation marks and under-
lining to indicate titles of published works; the manuscripts themselves, of course, may not include that
information. I have added additional comments in
brackets.

Description

The Roger Zelazny Papers contain biographical and
background material, correspondence, writings, publications of the Science Fiction Writers of America, and
published material. Contained in the biographical and

background material, 1954, 1966-1968, is published matter relating to science fiction conventions and activities in which Mr. Zelazny participated, as well as financial records.

Correspondence, 1954-1968, most of it incoming [i.e., the letters are those written to Zelazny; very seldom is there any copy of his reply], is from publishers, literary agents, science fiction writers, and fans. Arranged chronologically, much of the correspondence relates to Mr. Zelazny's writings and science fiction activities, including one group of letters from a fourth-grade class which read "Susi's Magic Pterodactyl" [an unpublished juvenile Zelazny had tried on the students], placed at the end of the correspondence.

Important correspondents include, Ace Books, Inc., 1966-1968; Amazing-Fantastic Publications [sic], 1965-1966; Ballantine Books, Inc., 1968; Lloyd Biggle, Jr., 1963, 1966-1967; James Blish, 1966, 1968; Philip K. Dick, 1967; Doubleday and Company, Inc., 1964, 1966-1968; Faber and Faber Ltd., 1966-1968; Fantasy and Science Fiction, 1962-1968; Galaxy, 1968; Alma Hill, 1964-1967; Hugo Awards, 1964, 1968; Damon Knight, 1965-1967; Robert P. Mills, 1964-1966; Henry Morrison, 1967-1968; New Worlds, 1965-1968; Frederick Pohl, 1963, 1966-1968; Rex Stout, 1968; Ziff-Davis Publishing Company, 1962-1965. A list of this correspondence with exact dates may be found in the first folder of Box 1.

Writings, 1965-1968, are composed of typescripts, holographs, and printed materials, and are arranged alphabetically by title under the divisions of fiction, non-fiction and poetry. Many of the manuscripts are not dated, and those not titled are arranged alphabetically by the first lines of the manuscripts. Many of Mr. Zelazny's prize-winning stories are contained in this series.

Material from Science Fiction Writers of America
consists of the Secretary-Treasurer's Handbook by Mr.
Zelazny and Nebula Award Stories 3, co-edited [sic] by
Mr. Zelazny. Published material, 1965-1967, includes
fanzine magazines (magazines published by fans and ama-
teurs in the science fiction field).

Gift of Roger Zelazny, Dec., 1966; April and Aug.
1968.

SHELF LIST

Box 1   Biographical and Background Material

Published material, 1966-1968; correspondence,
August 1967
Financial records, 1954, 1967-1968

Correspondence

1954-1965
1966
1967

Box 2   1968 [Files much more voluminous in later
years; as noted above, very few of Zelazny's
replies included.]
Undated
"Susi's Magic Pterodactyl," February 4, 1965

Writings

Addresses
Untitled, holograph, n.d.   [Triple Fan
Fair speech; see C13.]
Fiction
"And call me Conrad," original typescript
revised, 164p. [See A40.]
"Angel, dark angel," original typescript
revised, 12p. [See A60.]

Beside the Vedra, typescript carbon (see
Lord of light, Chapter 6), 56p. [See
A63.]

"The Borgia hand," original typescript revised, 4p. [See A12.]

Clementowicz & the commisar, holograph revised, 13p. ["On the Road to Spenolba";
see A10.]

Co Nestor's fever (The world, the deeble,
and Uncle Sidney's rock collection),
original typescript revised, 5p.
["Collector's Fever"; see A27.]

"Corrida," original typescript revised, 3p.
[See A74.]

Damnation Alley
Incomplete published material, revised,
3p.
Publicity, repro. annotated; correspondence, n.d. [See A65.]

Box 3   "Dismal light," original typescript revised, 15p. [See A70.]

"Divine madness," original typescript
revised, 8p. [See A49; also note that
portions of this are typed on the back
of a typescript of This Immortal.]

"The doors of his face, the lamps of his
mouth," original typescript revised,
37p.
In Fantasy and science fiction, Vol. 28,
no. 3 (March 1965), p. 4-30; revised;
1 drawing [marked for reprint in Ace
collection Four for Tomorrow (see A54);
the drawing is Jack Gaughan's spot
illustration.]
Publicity, published material, 1966-1968
The dream master, book reviews, March 25,
April 14, 1968; correspondence, n.d.
[note from Terry Carr, Ace editor.]

"Final dining," original typescript
revised, 12p. [See A41.]

"For a Brbath [sic] I tarry," holograph
   revised, 40p. [See A46.]
Four for tomorrow
   Book review; correspondence, n.d.
   Introduction by Theodore Sturgeon,
   original typescript revised; correspond-
   ence, n.d., 11p.
   [See A54.]
"The furies," published material, revised;
   1 drawing, 15p. [As in the case of
   "The Doors of His Face, The Lamps of His
   Mouth," above, this has been prepared
   for typesetting for Four for Tomorrow.]
"The graveyard heart," typescript carbon
   revised; 1 drawing, 15p. [See "The
   Doors of His Face, The Lamps of His
   Mouth" above; see also A26.]
Hand of the master, original typescript
   revised, 3p. [Opening: "I shook
   hands around and left the Senate
   Chamber. . . ."]
He yt moves (these bones)
   Original typescript revised, 9p.
   Typescript carbon, 13p.
["He That Moves"; see A69. File also in-
   cludes a copy of WSFA Journal, no. 51,
   on page 2 of which Banks Mebane mentions
   story.]
"He who shapes" (see the Ides of Octemeber)
   Draft A, original typescript, 8p.
   Draft B, original typescript, 48p.
   Draft C, original typescript, 15p.
   Draft D, original typescript, 2p.
   Draft E, original typescript, 2p.
   Part III, original typescript revised,
   37p.
   [See A33; most of the above appear to be
   insertions, to bring magazine version up
   to novel length.]

"Horseman!," original typescript revised,
3p. [See A6.]
The hounds of sorrow
Original typescript revised, 8p.
Typescript carbon, 11p.
[Opening: "When Mattie goes to sleep,
I'm going to blow his goddam head off."]
"The house of the hanged man," typescript
carbon, 5p. [See A52.]
Hunt down the happy wallaby, holograph
revised, 45p.
["The Furies"; see A37.]
The Ides of Octember (see He Who Shapes)
Synopsis, original typescript revised,
2 p. [Vastly different than published
version.]
Original typescript revised, 96p.
[See A33.]
In the dry of Capricorn, original typescript
revised, 3p. ["Monologue for Two"; see
A18.]

Box 4   The insider, typescript carbon revised, 6p.
[Opening: "Take Chthulu for an
example. . . ."]
The Juan's thousandth," original typescript
revised, 9p. [Opening: "Starfall and
haven. . . ."]
"The keys to December," original typescript
revised, 24 p. [See A51.]
"King Solomon's ring," original typescript
revised, 24p. [See A22.]
"A knight for Merytha," original typescript
revised, 10p. [See A62.]
"The last inn on the road," typescript car-
bon revised, 7p. [See A66.]
Lord of Hellwell (see Lord of Light)
Typescript carbon, 55p. [See A63.]

Lord of light
Chapter 7, typescript carbon, 51p.
Printer's copy, typescript carbon anno-
tated, ca. 1967
Pages 1-178
Pages 179-385
Final galley proof revised, ca. 1967,
90 p.
Page proof, annotated, ca. 1967, 84p.
Page proof, annotated, ca. 1967, 84p.
Book reviews, published material, 1967-
1968; correspondence, April 1968
[See A63.]

Box 5   "Love is an imaginary number"
Original typescript revised, 7p.
Publicity, published material, 1968;
correspondence, January 8, 1968
[See A44.]
Maitreya, typescript carbon (see Lord of
light, Chapter 1), 54p. [See A63.]
"The man who loved the Faioli," original
typescript revised; correspondence,
January 16, 1967. [See A58.]
"Mine is the kingdom," original typescript
revised, 7p. [See A21.]
"The misfit," original typescript revised,
6p. [See A23.]
"Moonless in Byzantium," original type-
script revised, 6p. [See A9.]
Morning of the scarlet swinger, original
typescript revised, 16p. [Opening:
"Murdock sped across the Great Western
Road Plain."]
"The new pleasure," typescript carbon, 5p.
[See A30.]
"The night has nine hundred ninety-nine
eyes," typescript carbon, 4p. [See
A31.]

Nine princes in amber, original typescript
    revised, 162p.
    Notes, original typescript, June 27,
    1968
    [See A87.]
"Nine starships waiting," original type-
    script revised, 40p. [See A13.]
None but the lonely hart, original type-
    script revised, 7p. ["Threshold of the
    Prophet"; see A19.]
Of time and the yan, original typescript
    revised, 4p. ["Of Time and Yan"; see
    A38.]
Party set, original typescript revised,
    58p. ["The Graveyard Heart"; see A26.]
"Passage to Dilfar," holograph revised, 8p.
    [See A34.]
"Passion play," original typescript revised,
    4p. [See A7.]
Power & light, original typescript revised,
    6p. ["Lucifer"; see A28.]
The powers of heaven, original typescript
    revised, 54p. (see Lord of light,
    chapter 5) [See A63.]
Prelude in the house of the dead, original
    typescript revised, 130p. [Creatures of
    Light and Darkness; see A80.]
"A rose for Ecclesiastes," in Fantasy and
    science fiction, pp. 5-35; 1 drawing,
    16p. [See "The Doors of His Face, The
    Lamps of His Mouth" above; see also
    A54.]
Snap dragon man (Walker in the Earth),
    original typescript revised, 3p.
    [Opening: "It was a morning as green
    and golden as a poem by Dylan
    Thomas. . . ."]
"Song of the blue Baboon," typescript
    carbon, 7p.

Box 6 Original typescript revised, 6p.
[See A72.]
Song of the witch's daughter, typescript
carbon, 11p. ["Thelinde's Song"; see
A39.]
Spaceman's lament, original typescript
revised, 8p. ["Circe Has Her Problems";
see A14.]
"Stainless steel leech," original type-
script revised, 5p. ["The Stainless
Steel Leech"; see A16.]
"The teacher [sic] rode a wheel of fire,"
original typescript revised, 5p. [See
A8.]
There shall be no moon!, original typescript
revised, 11p. [Opening: "'Percy?'"
"'Yes, George?'"]
"A thing of terrible beauty," original
typescript revised, 11p. [See A17.]
This immortal
Printer's copy, typescript carbon anno-
tated; correspondence, 233p.
Book reviews, repro., December 1967–
1968, 14p.
Publicity, published material; corre-
spondence, n.d., 14p.
[See A47.]
"This moment of storm [sic]," original
typescript revised, 30p. [See A48.]
"This mortal mountain," original typescript
revised, 39p. [See A55.]
Through a glass greenly, original typescript
revised, 4p. [Opening: "Where did you
ever get it, Lundy?"]
Time of night in the 7th room
Original typescript revised, 6p.
Typescript carbon, 8p.
[Opening: "This is the story Cricet and
Lord Chek of the snail fort."]

Tomorrow stuff
  Holograph revised, 6p.
  Typescript carbon, 8p.
  [Essay on writing science fiction.
  Opening: "It is always difficult to say
  why a writer writes."]
A turn unstoned, original typescript re-
    vised, 17p. ["A Museum Piece"; see A20.]
The window washer, original typescript
    revised, 11p. [Opening: "It was when
    he noticed that the window washer was
    not using a safety belt. . . ."]
Zindrome of negative speed, original type-
    script revised, 8p. ["The Great Slow
    Kings"; see A25.]
Untitled [Quotation marks in this section
surround the first words of the text. I have
added the titles of published works.]
  "And I knew of all men [Niccolo
    Machiavelli]," holograph revised, 2p.
  "The bell drowned his every seventh word,"
    holograph revised, 1p. [This and next
    five fragments appear to be related to
    Damnation Alley (see A82), probably
    written as part of expansion of magazine
    version to novel length.
  "The bell that rang again," original type-
    script revised, 3p.
  "The bell was ringing," original typescript
    revised, 3p.
  "Evelyn listened," original typescript
    revised, 6p.
  "Gregory Rumford listened to the bell,"
    original typescript revised, 3p.
  "He disembarked in New York Harbor,"
    original typescript revised, 3p. ["Stow-
    away"; see A71. Zelazny says this was
    written approximately same time as
    Damnation Alley, working same theme.]
  "He heard a chuckle," holograph revised,
    7p. [Insert for Damnation Alley.]

"He wondered," original typescript revised,
13p. [Insert for The Dream Master.]

"Hell Tanner and Jerry Potter walked,"
holograph revised, 2p. [Insert for
Damnation Alley.]

"Henry Soames, M.D., knew," holograph
revised, 2p. [Insert for Damnation
Alley.]

"It reared, roared, writhed," original
typescript revised, 3p.

"It was on the Pa. Tpk.," holograph
revised, 2p.

"Life is a thing," original typescript
revised, 153p. [Isle of the Dead; see
A77.]

"One of the mechanics approached them,"
original typescript revised, 15 p.
[Insert for Damnation Alley.]

"Setting without characters," original
typescript revised, 3p.

"There was a burst of light," original
typescript revised, 3p.

"What's the last you heard," holograph
revised, 3p. [Insert for Damnation
Alley.]

"Within the theater," original typescript
revised, 3p. [Insert for Damnation
Alley.]

Untitled fragments, original typescript
revised, and holograph, 11p. [Isle of
the Dead insert and summary differing
somewhat from published version--open-
ing: "Luke Shimbo, retired, is the only
human worldscaper in the business."]

Non-fiction

(Answers to eleven questions about science
fiction), original typescript revised,
10p. [For Double:Bill; see C3.]

(Bibliography of science fiction criticism),
original typescript revised, 2p.

[General, not relating primarily to
Zelazny himself.]

Christianity and courtly love, the allego-
ries of opposites, typescript carbon,
12p. [Winner of the Holden essay com-
position while Zelazny was a student at
Western Reserve University.]

Fanzine bibliography (not complete), two
typescripts, one revised, 5p.
[Apparently prepared for WSFA Journal;
see note at end of Part D.]

I just received NYAR II, re: Alexei
Panshin, original typescript revised,
3p. ["De Gustibus"; see C3.]

I never met Cordwainer Smith, re: Cordwainer Smith, original typescript, 3p.
["Cordwainer Smith," see C19.]

In praise of his spirits, noble and otherwise, (foreword), original typescript
revised; typescript carbon annotated,
10p. ["Foreword: In Praise of His
Spirits, Noble and Otherwise" to From
the Land of Fear (Ellison); see C12.]

Box 7   On writing and stories," original typescript
revised; typescript carbon, 7p. [See C9.]

"The search for the historical L. Sprague de
Camp or, the compleat dragon-catcher,"
original typescript revised; typescript
carbon; correspondence, December 2, 1965,
10p. [See C7.]

The world of z, this being in the nature of
a nonintroduction to the volume in hand,
original typescript revised, 3p. ["Introduction" to A Private Cosmos (Farmer);
see C16.]

Poetry

Avalanches, The thing that on the highways,
and Fire snakes and the moon, holograph,
1p.

Between you and I, holograph revised, 1p.

131

Bok, holograph revised and original typescript, 2p.

"The cat licks her coat," holograph, 1p.
[See B21.]

"Cross Caribbean" (In memoriam, Hart Crane),
original typescript, 1p. [See B15.]

"Dim," holograph, 2p. [See B27.]

Dreams, dreams, holograph revised, 1p.

I never met a traveller from an antique
land, holograph revised, 1p.

I was born, holograph, 1p.

"Moonsong," holograph revised, 1p. [See
B28.]

Pelias waking within the S.C., holograph
revised, 1p.

"Pyramid," holograph revised, 1p. [See B20.]

Reply, original typescript revised, 2p.

See you later, maybe, holograph revised,
1p.

"There is always a poem," holograph revised,
1p. [See B23.]

This book is dedicated to, holograph
revised, 1p. [Actually, draft of dedi-
cation to Bob Silverberg, in Nebula
Award Stories Three; see A75.]

Notes, original typescript and holograph,
13p. [Hodgepodge of jottings, including
family tree for characters in Creatures
of Light and Darkness, draft of comments
for back covers of Ace Specials, etc.]

The great selchie of San Francisco Bay,
original typescript revised, 4p. [Play
script.]

Science Fiction Writers of America
Nebula award stories 3, edited by
R. Zelazny and Robert Silverberg [sic].
Secretary-treasurer's handbook, by R.
Zelazny
Holograph, 8p.
Draft A, original typescript revised,
7p. [Begins on p. 4.]

Draft B, original typescript revised, 8p.
Draft C, original typescript revised, 8p.
Draft D, original typescript revised, 17p.
Draft E, typescript revised, 12p.
Draft F, repro. of original typescript, 43p.
[See C21.]

Published Material

Fanzine magazines, 1965-1967
Argh, vol. 1, no. 1, March 1963
Degler, no. 168, February 10, 1967
Eye, no. 21, January 1967
Focal point, no. 1, January 8, 1965
Merry marvel messenger, c1966
Panhelion, no. 3, November-December 1967
W.S.F.A. journal
no. 4, July 1965
no. 17, March 1966
no. 22, May 1966
no. 29, September 1966
no. 39, mid-March 1967
no. 40, April 1967
no. 41, mid-April 1967
no. 47, October 1967
Writer's exchange, n.d.
[With the exception of The WSFA Journal, no. 47 (see D27), these fanzines contain no substantial material by or about Zelazny. They appear to be merely fanzines he had accumulated--his living in Baltimore would account for the number of WSFA Journals.]

II. University of Maryland Baltimore County

Part of the following description is based on a
letter from Ms. Binnie Syril Braunstein, Assistant Co-
ordinator, Business and Bibliographic Services (and
Curator of Science Fiction), supplemented by a telephone
call from Ms. Braunstein during which she looked through
the material. Such material is noted with an asterisk.
The bulk of the description is based on personal inspection of the assortment of manuscripts and papers then in
the keeping of Lloyd Curry Rare Books and since acquired
by UMBC.

The file of correspondence at UMBC, 2-3000 public-
private letters, is exceptionally valuable in that most
letters are paper clipped to carbons of Zelazny's replies. The run of business and personal correspondence
extends from 1970 to 1976.

The collection contains the following manuscripts,
arranged alphabetically.

> "Author's Choice"--carbon. [See C36.]
> Book review of Rendezvous with Rama--rough-typed
>   [mixture of typing and handwriting]; carbon.
>   ["A Sense of Wonder"; see C38.]
> Book review of The Times of London Anthology of
>   Detective Stories--carbon. ["Who Done It?
>   And why?"; see C39.]
> Bridge of Ashes--rough-typed; final carbons;
>   final marked for printer; also synopsis writ-
>   ten for publishers [differing somewhat in
>   order of sections from printed version;
>   opening section came after da Vinci incarna-
>   tion]; some clippings and research material.
>   [See A106.]
> *The Doors of His Face, The Lamps of His Mouth,
>   and Other Stories--galley proofs (with cor-
>   rections); page proofs; setting copy/reader's
>   galleys (with production notes); setting copy,
>   part 2. [See A89.]

Doorways in the Sand--installment synopses [for
Analog serialization] rough-typed and final
carbon; summary for Harpers' editors; final
ms. marked for printer; galleys. [See A100,
A102.]

"The Engine at Heartspring's Center"--rough
handwritten; carbon. [See A96.]

"The Force that Through the Circuit Drives the
Current"--rough-typed; carbon. [See A108.]

"The Game of Blood and Dust"--rough-typed; final
carbon. [See A99.]

The Guns of Avalon--carbons; galleys. [See A92.]

*The Guns of Avalon--final draft of ms; carbon
copy of final, carbon proof; mockup of dustjacket; correspondence.

The Hand of Oberon--synopses rough-typed; marked
for printer; edited galleys. [See A104,
A105.]

"Home is the Hangman"--rough-typed; final carbon.
[See A101.]

Introduction to "The Man Who Loved the Faioli"--
rough-handwritten; carbon. [See C43.]

Introduction to Philip K. Dick: Electric
Shepherd--handwritten; final carbon. [See
C45.]

"Jack of Shadows"--synopsis for F&SF serializa-
tion, carbon. [See A90.]

"'Kjwalll'kje'k'koothaïlll'kje'k'"--carbon.
[See A95.]

*"'Kjwalll'kje'k'koothaïlll'kje'k'"--original ms.
and final draft; carbon; correspondence.
[Ms. Braunstein reports that part of this is
typed on the back of pages from another manuscript, which appears to be a detective story.]

"$Legislation$"--carbon. [Message to SFWA, on
change of tax laws concerning deductions for
mss donations.]

"Love is an Imaginary Number"--carbon. [See
A44.]

"The Man Who Loved the Faioli"--carbon. [See
A58.]

<u>My Name is Legion</u>--precis, handwritten; carbons.
   [<u>See</u> A103.]
"Science Fiction and its Ideas in Six Digressions"--rough-handwritten; carbon. ["Ideas,
   Digressions and Daydreams: The Amazing
   Science Fiction Machine"; <u>see</u> C46.]
"Sign of the Unicorn"--rough-typed; final carbon;
   galleys; prefatory essay ("An Essay in Amber")
   [to introduce serial in <u>Galaxy</u>], rough-typed,
   carbons; segment synopses [for <u>Galaxy</u>], rough-
   typed, final carbons. [<u>See</u> A97.]
"Some Parameters of Science Fiction"--rough-
   typed; carbon. ["Some Science Fiction
   Parameters: A Biased View"; <u>see</u> C44.]
*<u>Today We Choose Faces</u>--carbons of original ms.
   (including correspondence with publishers,
   some minor corrections of typos). [<u>See</u> A93.]
<u>To Die in Italbar</u>--final carbon. [<u>See</u> A94.]
*<u>To Die in Italbar</u>--Xerox of Doubleday copy;
   copyedited ms. (question and answer correspondence enclosed); galley proofs; page
   proofs.
"Up Against the Wall, Roger Zelazny!"--carbon.
   [<u>See</u> C34.]
Untitled essay on sf's development--carbon, 6pp.

UMBC also own Monteleone's M.A. thesis on Zelazny,
   D151.

Indexes

Index to Primary Works

First citation after each title indicates the section in which it is listed (i.e., whether it is fiction, poetry, or non-fiction). Following citations cover comments in Zelazny's writing or comments, reviews, or substantial references by someone else.

Index to Secondary Sources

Anonymous, untitled writings having been included already in Index A, this index covers only other pieces. Titles of book review columns or group review essays are not included.

Hillman, Martin, D21
"Hoarde of Write: On Roger Zelazny," D121
Holmberg, John-Henri, D61
Hooks, Wayne, D256
Hubbard, Gary N., D62
Hunter, Stephen, D125

Imaginary Worlds, D139
"Impertinent Editorial Aside Concerning the Parentage
    of the Princes of Amber," D144
"Introduction" to "Auto-da-fe," D18
"Introduction" to The Dream Master, D236
"Introduction" to Four for Tomorrow, D31
"Introduction" to Isle of the Dead, D225
"Introduction" to Today We Choose Faces, D296
"Irresistable Schlog Meets Immovable Critic," D259

The Jewel-Hinged Jaw, D249
Johnson, W., D146
Jonas, Gerald, D211
Jones, M., D212
Justice, K., D213

Keller, Donald G., D84, D85, D86
Ketterer, David, D165
King, Tappan, D217
Klein, Jay Kay, D22

[Laber, J. M. C.], D23
[Laker, J. H. C.], D39
Last, Martin, D214, D215
"'Les Mots': Never Question Roses," D47
Lewis, S., D257
"Lies, All Lies," D210
Livingston, W., D147
"Lord of Light," D300
"Love is Madness," D42
"Lunacon/Eastercon 1967," D22